Memories of Che

Memories of
CHE

Edited by Guillermo Cabrera Alvarez

Translated from the Spanish by
Jonathan Fried

Lyle Stuart Inc.   **Secaucus, New Jersey**

Published by Lyle Stuart, Inc.
120 Enterprise Ave., Secaucus, N.J. 07094
In Canada; Musson Book Company
a division of General Publishing Co. Limited
Don Mills, Ontario

Manufactured in the United States of America

Library of Congress Cataloging-in-Publication Data

Memories of Che.

    1. Guevara, Ernesto, 1928-1967--Anecdotes.
2. Guevara, Ernesto, 1928-1967--Friends and
associates. 3. Latin America--Biography.
4. Guerrillas--Latin America--Biography.
I. Cabrera Alvarez, Guillermo, 1943-   .
II. Fried, Jonathan L.
F2849.22.G85M43 1987   980'.035'0924   87-6450
ISBN 0-8184-0385-3

To those who will be like him.

ACKNOWLEDGMENTS

I owe much to those whose conversations are recorded throughout this work, and to my friend, Emilio Surí, who collaborated in many of the following pages.

Contents

Memories of Che

INTRODUCTION

I was five years old when Ernesto "Che" Guevara was born in Argentina in 1927. We met for the first time 33 years later.

This is how that first meeting occurred.

I was in Cuba for the May Day celebration in 1960. Mary Louise, my first wife, and I intended to stay only three days. On the 4th day she flew back to New York to care for our children, Rory and Sandy. I remained for another ten days.

I met a journalist and writer named Carleton Beals. Beals was a hero in Cuba for a book that had become a classic: *Crime of Cuba*. (Currently he is a hero in Nicaragua for his book *With Sandino in Nicaragua*.)

We both got the usual stalling excuses when we requested a meeting with Fidel.

"Let's talk to Che," Carleton said. "He's now President of the National Bank. Why, I'll never understand!"

We taxied to the Banco Nacional. Unlike most other government halls and offices, its waiting room was conspicuously lacking in revolutionary literature and posters. On the coffee table were copies of *The Economist*.

We sat on a couch while a secretary hurried into Che's office to announce our presence. Che's door was ajar. She hurried out

15

again and explained that Major Guevara couldn't see us. He was "too busy running the bank."

I accepted that. Carleton didn't. As if making a speech to thousands, Carleton replied in an angry stentorian voice, "The Commandante has time to see Robert Considine, representative of the reactionary Hearst press, but no time for journalists who are sympathetic to the Revolution!"

In less than a minute, Che was at the door, smiling.

"Come in," he said in Spanish.

The two of us spent the next several hours with him. Then, at his suggestion, the three of us went to the Floridita for dinner.

It was for me a memorable meeting. Che was a memorable man. He was graceful, quick, sensitive and perceptive. We liked each other immediately even though some of my questions seemed to make him uncomfortable.

In 1959, probably ninety-eight percent of all Cubans had welcomed the victory of the Revolution against the American-supported dictator, Fulgencio Batista.

Time had passed and not all hopes and dreams had been realized. An uneasy balance of power had developed. Intellectuals, students, the unions and the old underground groups aligned themselves behind the newspaper *Revolucion*, which was edited by a brilliant decent man named Carlos Franqui.

On the other side was Raul Castro, the army and the old-line communists.

That evening at dinner Che indicated to us that he believed the United States rather than Fidel would shape Cuba's destiny.

"If your leaders are smart enough to design an accommodation, Cuba will become a democratic socialist country similar to Tito's Yugoslavia. But I doubt that they are smart enough—and I believe they'll give this Revolution to us by default."

By "us" he obviously meant the Marxists.

I was reminded of Che's words on a subsequent visit to Cuba when a man I knew stopped me on the street.

He was Waldo Medina, now the Chief Prosecutor of the Cuban Supreme Court. He was a competent lawyer, and to me symbolized the middle class that supported Fidel.

Introduction

The paste was still fresh on the billboards throughout Cuba that proclaimed, "The Cuban Revolution is Humanist—not Communist."

The United States would change all that. It had suddenly and flatly refused to refine oil for Cuba. Without oil, nothing would run: not factories, not automobiles, not elevators. Everything would grind to a halt and the Cuban Revolution would collapse.

Russia came to the rescue with a fleet of oil tankers.

Medina, with tears in his eyes asked, "Mr. Stuart, why is your President handing this Revolution to the Communists?"

I asked him what he meant.

He said, "If you're a little fellow and a big man tries to burn down your home and another big man comes to assist you, you accept the help gratefully. You don't stop to question the politics or religion of your savior. The United States is trying to destroy us. The Soviets are saving us. You're giving the Communists a victory they didn't earn and don't deserve!"

I believe (despite all the later revelations about CIA plots to poison Fidel Castro) that the United States wanted Fidel in power. He was the enemy but he was "our" enemy. We understood him. We could cope with him. We couldn't be sure of other revolutionary groups, some of which were forming even then in the mountains.

In that belief I was in harmony with Carlos Franqui who wrote in his book, *Family Portrait with Fidel:* "The CIA which is overtly Fidel's enemy has always been his potential ally. The CIA has its own way of doing business. It wanted to control [any] counterrevolution and to retake Cuba on its own terms, using former Batista supporters or recruits from the bourgeoisie. The result was that, for the Cuban people, opposition and counter-revolution became synonyms."

In an interview in *Look* magazine that year (November 8, 1960) Che was quoted as saying, "What lies ahead depends greatly on the United States. With the exception of our agrarian reform, which the people of Cuba desired and initiated themselves, all of our radical measures have been in direct response to direct aggressions

17

by powerful monopolies of which your county is the chief exponent. U.S. pressure on Cuba has made necessary the 'radicalization' of the Revolution. To know how much farther Cuba will go, it will be easier to ask the U.S. government how far it plans to go."

On that day in May, Commandante Guevara didn't sound as antagonistic to my country as I'd been told he was.

When I suggested agrarian reform and the seizure of American property were moving so quickly that America might send in the marines, he replied with a variation of a slogan I was to hear frequently that year: "Let them come here. They'll stay here."

As I continued to visit Cuba, sometimes as often as three times in a year, I came to admire him more and more. He was likeable. He had a twinkle in his eye and he had a quick wit.

One day my friend Gloria Marsan and I met him in midafternoon at Bodeguita del Medio.

"Gloria, why are you here with Mr. Stuart?" he asked. "You should be at work."

"Che why are *you* here? *You* should be at work," Gloria retorted.

"Touché!" he replied with a chuckle.

What qualities set him apart from other men?

Certainly he was different. In my lifetime I have known only a few people with a magnetism that could spellbind an audience. I once observed singer Al Jolson at Manhattan Beach in Brooklyn. It was raining and Jolson held an umbrella over his head with one hand and a microphone in the other. And two thousand people stood captivated and allowed themselves to get drenched while he sang for more than an hour in the pouring rain.

I attended some of Maurice Chevalier's many "farewell" appearances. He would saunter out to the center of the stage looking grim. He would stare at the usually sold-out audience. And then he would break into his smile and a current of excitement ran through the theater.

Introduction

Che had this effect on people. I remember a garden party at the Swiss Embassy given by Ambassador Emil Stadelhofer. Dozens of people stood chatting, cocktails in hand. My back was to the entrance but I knew, without looking, that Che had arrived for you could literally feel the electricity.

It's one of those things you had to experience to understand.

He was charged with magnetism and charm and strength and—yes, beauty. I.F. Stone once described him as "the most beautiful man I ever met."

"Che" is an affectionate way of saying "you" in Argentina. (I have been told it also means "our" and thus "our Guevara.") Actually, Che appears to have been given this nickname in Guatemala when he was in his mid-twenties.

Che Guevara came from a *bourgeois* family in Rosario, the second largest city in Argentina. His father, Ernesto Guevara Lynch, operated a *maté* farm near Cordoba in a place called Alta Gracia. The father was active in left-wing politics as was his wife, Celia de la Serna, who owned the farm. His father had Irish blood through his mother, while his own Mother was Spanish in origin. He had four brothers and sisters.

Che's political awareness may have developed from his association with several friends whose parents were exiled or killed in the Spanish Civil War. And then there was his odyssey in Peru and Chile on motorbike and on foot—described in this volume.

Hugh Thomas in his book *Cuba: The Pursuit of Freedom*, describes Che in 1955 as "a revolutionary but not necessarily a Marxist. He recognized that changing the means of production is the father to political change. He believed in the 'purgative effects of revolution' believing (as he later put it) that 'revolution cleanses men...'"

Thomas described Guevara's qualities of leadership as "scarcely less than those of Castro himself, though they were more analytical and less intuitive."

When I was a reporter with International News Service, the company's slogan was: "Get it first, but first get it right!" Experience also taught me to accept quickly another newsman adage: "Believe nothing you hear and only half of what you see."

19

I was reminded of this in Havana in the mid 1960s. At that time I interviewed Jacob Arbenz who had been ousted as the legally elected President of Guatemala by a CIA-financed and directed plot.

Newspapers and magazines had written again and again about how Marxist Guevara had been the "brains" and "strategy director" of the Arbenz regime.

I questioned Arbenz about this. My interpreter translated his reply. On the chance that my question hadn't been understood, I asked him the same question many different ways. (I still retain the tape of that interview.) His responses were consistent.

Arbenz understood that Major Guevara had been a clerk in the Guatemalan government but regretted that he had never had the pleasure of meeting him until this visit to Havana!

I published the interview in my monthly paper, *The Independent.* Then I started a one-man campaign to "correct" the press. With the exception of *Newsweek,* all the periodicals stopped the inaccuracy. Only *Newsweek* continued to identify Guevara as "the brain of the Arbenz government." Finally I wrote directly to Philip Graham, *Newsweek's* publisher.

Graham apologized with a charming note. He assured me that, effective immediately, *Newsweek* would not again publish the lie.

It didn't.

Guevara is said to have come out of his experience in Guatemala quite hostile to the United States. I'm sure this was true, but in my presence he was always diplomatic with me, expressing only intellectual criticism rather than anger.

In the Sierras, Che headed the medical corps. He was a physician, inspired to be one when, as a young man, he witnessed the painful death of his grandmother from cancer. His revolutionary feelings came from what he saw of misery in one Central American country after another.

Eventually he made the decision that would shape the remainder of his life. Caught in an enemy ambush, he described the alternatives: "On one side I had my knapsack full of med-icines, and on the other, an ammunition box. I couldn't carry both: they were too heavy. I took the ammunition. In doing that I made a clear choice."

Che led a handful of fighters to defeat Batista's heavily equipped army in the battle of Santa Clara. It was this defeat that unseated Batista and forced him to flee. Keep in mind that six months before this victory there were fewer than six hundred revolution-aries in the mountains and they faced a military force of more than 35,000 men, equipped with the most modern USA-made weaponry.

(Two years later, Fulgencio Batista published his own version of history, *Mi Respuesta*. He sent me a personally autographed copy from Spain. He told me I was being misled or I wouldn't show sympathy for the Cuban Revolution.)

Journalist Bob Taber observed that Che "had little use for grin-gos, journalists, business men, hustlers of any sort, politicians."

Whenever Che and I would meet, he would announce with a smile, "Photographs, yes. But no questions!"

My questions were too direct. It was clear to me that he was not always in accord with Fidel's cha-cha-cha brand of Marxism. Gradually, too, it was apparent that he was becoming critical of some things Soviet.

Carlos Franqui observed, "Che had always declared himself to be a Communist, but his brand of communism never convinced Fidel, who recognized Che's independence of character and his sense of morality."

Che himself admitted, "I was the first to support the Cuban Communist Party, and later I became a determined anti-party man."

Indeed, when he quarreled with the Soviet Union it was obvious that he cared more about integrity than about his own career.

People in political life, no matter what the system, are often torn between their sense of justice and their individual comfort; between their ideals and their appetite.

Che overcame these contradictions and became an expression of a living ideal.

Fidel Castro enjoyed comforts and good living. Che was an ascetic.

One example: With the triumph of the Revolution, its leaders set their own salaries. These averaged between 750 pesos to 1,000 pesos a month. (A peso was then equal to a U.S. dollar.) Che was austere: he took only 250 pesos.

Che Guevara suffered from a debilitating asthma from early childhood. A young Cuban writer told me about being with Che in a volunteer group that was trucked outside of Havana to sugar fields for the *zafra* (sugar harvest). All able-bodied men in Cuba were expected to participate to meet a goal of ten million tons of sugar for the year.

Che cut with the rest of them but at one point, scarcely able to breathe because of his asthma, he staggered out to the road and sat quietly, trying to catch his breath.

When the truck with the volunteers was ready to return to Havana, Che insisted on remaining behind. He felt he "owed" an hour of additional cane cutting to make up for the time he'd been incapacitated by the asthma.

This from the man who was easily the second most popular figure in the Revolution and the third most powerful. (Fidel's brother, Raul, ranked second.)

It is the feeling of every journalist I know who covered Cuba (and of every savvy Cuban) that Che always underestimated his popularity in Cuba. As an Argentinian, he felt he could never trespass beyond a certain point. He was very wrong.

Che once remarked, "In the beginning was the bullet." He believed that the struggle for independence and self-determination was the first step.

He was pure in a way that few leaders are pure. He was dedicated. His concept of the *new man* faltered and failed when put to the test in Cuba.

Introduction

I will not dwell here on Che's concept of the Man of the Future—a man so idealistic that he would no longer use or need money. The dream seems far-fetched now. But who can say with certainty what a century will bring? Or even two centuries? And what are a couple of centuries in the infinite sands of time?

Transforming the world—transforming humans from being selfish and self-seeking to being genuinely concerned with the community of man—is a dream that may indeed take centuries to realize, if the human species doesn't destroy itself first.

Che tried to typify what he believed. He was generous, believed in humanity, and had a strong will and character.

Things change and the time would come when Che Guevara refused to become an echo of Moscow or even a reflection of Fidel. His usefulness was at an end to the Johnny-come-latelies who had replaced the 26th of July Revolutionary heroes.

One of Che's problems was that he insisted on talking in terms of Latin American revolution on a long-range scale instead of simply the Cuban Revolution.

Unlike Fidel, he was willing to admit mistakes. Unlike Fidel, he didn't revise history to suit current policy. Fidel depended on bureaucracy: Che loathed it.

Had Che lived, he would certainly have opposed the establishment of detention camps for homosexuals in the late 1960s. The infantile concept of "machismo" was never an overwhelming emotion with Che.

Carlos Franqui confronted Fidel, pulling him away from an important meeting, to demand the abolition of the camps. Franqui reminded Fidel that Julius Caesar, Fidel's number one hero, was a homosexual. Fidel agreed to close the camps but he never spoke to Franqui again. (Franqui left Cuba a short time later.)

A personal note.

The following scenario could never have happened had Che been alive in the 1980s. I have always been against secret police everywhere whether our CIA or the Russian KGB. I have also been a longtime opponent of imprisoning men and women for their political beliefs.

If someone disagrees with a regime and/or its policies he should be free to express himself in speech and in writing. One of Fidel Castro's demands in his speech to the court when he was a political prisoner* was for the granting of liberty to people who express views contrary to those of the government.

To allow people to say or write only that which is in harmony with the state is, of course, not freedom at all.

All governments have a right to protect themselves from terrorists. But though they have the power, they have no moral right to restrict the flow of words or ideas, spoken or on paper.

It was therefore natural for me to agree to assist French publishing executive Marie-Pierre Bay when she asked, on behalf of PEN, the international writers' association, if I would use whatever contacts I had in Havana to obtain freedom for a Cuban poet named Edmigio Lopez Castillo. Castillo was a prisoner in Combinado del Este prison outside of Havana.

My second wife Carole and I visited Cuba in early 1985. I was determined to confront every official I met on behalf of Castillo.

Armando Hart, a Revolutionary hero, had once been Minister of Education and was now Minister of Culture. He is also a member of the Politburo and of the Central Committee.

He promised to look into the matter.

The next evening we dined at Central Committee Headquarters at a special dinner given in our honor and hosted by Antonio (Tony) Perez Herrero.

Tony Herrero directed the ideologic aspects of the Revolution. He was Raul's companion during the fighting on the second front. Hart was a member of the 26th of July Movement. Herrero was a member of the Communist Party.

Unlike Hart, Herrero had heard of Castillo. For one thing, Cuban novelist Lisandro Otero, then Cultural Attaché in

---

History Will Absolve Me, published by Lyle Stuart Inc.

Moscow, had cabled a query about the man two days before our arrival in Havana.

I explained that Otero was responding to a letter from me.

Herrero said, "I must tell you that the man is not a poet and has never been a poet. Nor was he ever a journalist. He has done no work in Cuba. He is part of an organization of counter-revolutionaries. Nevertheless, in your honor, I am pleased to tell you he will be released shortly."

When we returned to the States, I conveyed the good news about "our" prisoner to Marie-Pierre Bay. A few weeks later a Cuban journalist visited the States and told me that Castillo had been released and "is living in Paris."

It wasn't until nearly a year later that I learned the prisoner had *not* been released. He was still in prison.

Tony Herrero was relieved from his post and sent on foreign missions.

I complained again and again to everyone I knew in Havana. The Second Secretary of the Cuban Mission to the United Nations asked for a meeting with me in Manhattan. We met and he explained that he had received orders from a "top person" in Cuba to investigate and learn who had lied to me and why they'd lied to me.

But, at this writing in February, 1987, Edmigio Lopez Castillo is still in a Cuban prison.

It has always been my impression that Fidel couldn't really deal with a sibling whose popularity challenged his own. His brother Raul, being colorless and mean-spirited, posed no threat. But I believe Fidel, consciously or unconsciously resented Che's self-confidence and popularity.

When a top Cuban is dispatched on foreign missions, the move represents a kind of disgrace and rejection. Years before, Che resigned his post as Minister of Industries to go to the Congo to fight on the side of the Kinshasa rebels. That was something he wanted to do.

In 1963, Che was sent on a series of trips. He went with a smile. Che never felt he was competing with Fidel.

So it was that when he disappeared in 1965, it was at first assumed that this was more political punishment.

For several months his whereabouts were unknown. There were rumors of a falling out with Fidel. He was a prisoner. He'd been shot. He was in Africa. No one knew if he'd gone, when he'd gone, where he'd gone, or why he'd gone.

Not untypically, our Central Intelligence Agency had made learning his whereabouts a top priority. A reliable CIA agent told me that one of the leading theories was that Che had taken some medicine for his asthma that had come from the Soviet Union and that had gone bad because of poor refrigeration. This had affected his mind. so the CIA theory went, and he was in a mental institution in the Soviet Union.

It was, of course, typical of the CIA's inability to be accurate on anything.

At this time, I had a five hour meeting with Fidel. Che's whereabouts were wrapped in mystery. At the same time, Cubans were being exhorted to "Follow the example of Camilo* and Che."

Fidel led a small caravan of cars to an army barracks two hours out of Havana. I'd asked for the meeting for Richard Eder of *The New York Times* and for Al Burt of the *Miami Herald*.

When the other reporters didn't raise what all felt was a 'delicate subject' I questioned Fidel about Che.

Yes, Che had given him a farewell letter in person. Fidel explained that for Che, revolution was a vocation. He had things he felt he wanted to do and that there were now people in Cuba trained to do some of the work that he had done.

"Is Che alive?" I asked.

"Yes, and living a very good life."

"Could he return to Cuba if he wanted to?"

"Of course," Fidel replied.

"Do you think he will ever return?"

---

*Camilo Cienfuegoes, a leader of the Revolution, disappeared shortly after its victory while on flight in a small plane. It was assumed that the plane crashed over the ocean. No remains were ever found.

"No."

"Fidel," I said, "I'm planning to publish a book of Che's speeches and I'd like you to write the introduction to it."

"I would be pleased and proud to write the introduction."

"Good," I said. "By the way, when I published the book I'd like to send copies to Che. Where should I address them?"

There was a twinkle in Fidel's eye when he replied, "Send them to me," he said, "I'll see that he gets them."

We all laughed. It was obvious to me from Fidel's relaxed good humor that, contrary to the wild rumors then extant, there had been no falling out, no bitter quarrel.

Che believed that only social revolution could change conditions in underdeveloped nations. The United States of America, the nation economically and industrially best able to narrow the gap between rich and poor, had instead become the most reactionary force of the last quarter of the twentieth century.

Che believed that revolution is a powerful moral force that compels its makers to develop an acute sense of social value.

He also wrote, "At the risk of sounding ridiculous, let me say that the true revolutionary is inspired by a great feeling of love.... It isn't enough to interpret the world—the world must be transformed. Humans must stop being the slaves and tools of their environment and transform themselves into architects of their own destiny."

"Other lands in the world claim the aid of my modest efforts," he wrote to Fidel in a letter dated January 4, 1965 and made public many months later. "I can do what is denied you because of your responsibility as the head of Cuba, and the time has come for us to separate.

"I remember at this hour many things: when I met you in Maria Antonia's house in Mexico: when you proposed that I join you; all the tensions of the preparations..."

"... I have so much to say to you and to our people but I feel it is unnecessary. Words could not express what I want and it's no use scribbling any more pages."

"I have lived magnificent days," Che wrote in his farewell letter to Fidel.

Eighty-three men comprised the expeditionary force that sailed on the *Granma* to invade Cuba from Mexico. Ernesto Guevara was the only foreigner among them and the only one in the group who had never seen the land he chose to liberate.

Only those who'd read his writings and listened to him talk knew that he felt the next logical place for Latin American revolution was in the mountains of Bolivia.

Che's struggle to help Third World people to free themselves from oppression, hunger, backwardness and waste was to end there. He was betrayed by Bolivian peasants whose language he couldn't speak, and shot on the instructions of the United States Central Intelligence Agency whose allegiance seems to be to tyranny and oppression.

This book was created by the Cubans at my request. Though it offers only scraps and fragments, my hope as publisher is that through these, one captures something of the beauty of the man, something of his essence.

Bertolt Brecht once wrote about a refugee who carried a brick with him wherever he went so people might know what his house had been like.

This book is a small stone, incomplete and imperfect, to show something of a man who died two decades ago and whose life will inspire men for a long time to come.

When Che met Fidel in Mexico in November, 1955, he was 26 years old.

When he was executed by the CIA in Bolivia in 1967, 13 years later, he was 39 years old.

Someone has written, "As in the case of Jose Martí or Lawrence of Arabia, failure has brightened, not dimmed, the legend."

Che Guevara was one of the few genuine heroes of our time. He was the last of the romantics.

LYLE STUART

Introduction

A POSTSCRIPT: In 1984, in a pure coincidence, Fidel Castro and I acquired Mercedes-Benz automobiles. They are the same color: grey. They are the same model: 500 SEL. There is one difference. Mine has a license plate that reads simply: CHE

1

NOT BECAUSE YOU'VE BEEN STILLED ARE YOU SILENCE

*Not because you have fallen
is your light less high.
A horse of fire
carries your guerrilla sculpture
in the wind and the clouds of the Sierra.
Not because you've been stilled are you silence.
And not because they burn you,
because they conceal you in the earth,
because they hide you
in cemeteries, forests, barren plateaus
will they prevent us from finding you,
Che Comandante,
friend.*

—NICOLÁS GUILLÉN

Autopsy Report

By military decree, on the 10th of October, 1967 an autopsy was performed on the corpse that was identified as that of Ernesto Guevara:

Age: approximately forty years. Race: white. Height: approximately 1.73 meters.

Curly brown hair; full grown mustache and beard, also curly; thick eyebrows; straight nose; thin lips; mouth half-open; teeth in good condition, with nicotine stains and missing the lower left premolar; light-blue eyes. Average physique.

Extremities: feet and hands well-preserved. Scar running almost the whole length of the back of the left hand.

In the general examination, the following injuries were found:

1. Bullet wound in the left clavicular region, exiting through the scapular region on the same side.

2. Bullet wound in the right clavicular region, causing a fracture.

3. Bullet wound in the region of the right rib cage.

4. Two bullet wounds in the region of the left rib cage, exiting through the back.

5. Bullet wound in the left pectoral region, between the ninth and tenth ribs, exiting through the left side.

6. Bullet wound in the middle third of the right leg.

7. Bullet wound passing through the middle third of the left thigh.

8. Bullet wound in the lower third of the right forearm, with a fracture of the cubitus.

When the thoracic cavity was opened, it was found that the first wound caused light damage to the vertex of the left lung.

The second damaged the subclavian vessels, the projectile becoming lodged in the second thoracic vertebra.

The third damaged the right lung, becoming lodged in the articulation of the ninth rib and the vertebral column.

The wounds indicated in point 4 caused light damage to the left lung.

The wound indicated in point 5 passed straight through the left lung.

The thoracic cavities, especially the right cavity, showed an abundant accumulation of blood.

When the abdomen was opened, no traumatic lesions were discovered, only distension of the intestines with gases and citrine liquid.

The cause of death was the wounds to the thorax and the consequent hemorrhaging.

Valle Grande, October 10, 1967
Dr. Abrahan Baptista
Dr. Martínez Caso

An Interview with Mario Terán by Journalist Jorge Canelas

"Who killed Che Guevara? Was it Major Prado Salmón?" I asked as soon as I thought I had softened him up.

"That's a story made up for fools. I killed Guevara because I'm remarkably brave. Two officers were afraid to do it; they refused, under the pretext that they were 'military men' and not 'hired assassins.' What nonsense!"

"Who gave the order to kill Guevara?"

"Don't you think you're being a little too inquisitive? That could be dangerous to your health."

I paid no attention to his cautioning advice and continued my line of questioning. I ordered more drinks for everyone. As an economist might say, it was an "investment" on which I expected a fair return.

"Barrientos and Ovando told General Joaquín Zenteno Anaya that Guevara mustn't be exhibited as a prisoner," Terán said. "They had to finish him off. According to subsequent rumors, the order came from Washington. I learned that the signal to do

33

him in was, 'Say hello to papa.' At that point Che's fate was sealed.

"Régis Debray had raised hell from his prison cell. What might Guevara have done? How could we let history repeat itself? Besides, we had to destroy the myth of the invincible guerrilla commander.

"From Vallegrande, he was brought to La Higuera. The political maneuvering was conspicuous. Officers and soldiers began to speculate left and right. No one dared 'say hello to papa.'

"Selich summoned me and told me to proceed with the measure. I had a few drinks and entered the room where Che lay, badly wounded. He had been shot in the leg."

"How did Guevara treat you?"

"He was arrogant. He admonished me and exhorted me to make haste. He knew he was on the threshold of death. I held my gun and fired into his left nipple. It was all over. Later I learned that Guevara had spit at Zenteno Anaya and Selich and had treated General Federico Arana Sernudo [subsequently ambassador to Venezuela] roughly."

I couldn't help but notice that Terán seemed to be struggling with his conscience. I was ready; the moment to attack had arrived.

"Are you proud of what you did?"

"I'm confused. Not only because I'm drunk but because at times I consider myself a hero of my country and other times I feel like a common murderer who doesn't deserve to live. I don't know whether I should feel proud or not. The only thing I know for sure is that I killed a man. From sergeant I was promoted to sergeant major, and Barrientos gave me money."

What One Journalist Had to Say

BUENOS AIRES, Oct. 14 (Prensa Latina)—Radio Portales has broadcast an interview with British journalist Richard Gott, who arrived in this capital from Santa Cruz, Bolivia.

Gott and Christopher Roper of Reuters were among the first to see the corpse of Che Guevara after it arrived in Valle Grande last Monday at 5 p.m. The guerrilla leader's body, tied to the landing gear of a military helicopter, was moved to Valle Grande from Higueras, where he was killed.

In the broadcast, Gott refers to a foreign man—bald, thirty years of age, dressed in olive green and carrying a machine gun over his shoulder—who tried to block his way. Gott believes the man was a C.I.A. agent.

Gott added that the foreigner spoke both Spanish and English well. "He left me with the impression that he was a Cuban working for the North Americans," he said.

"I even said to him in English. 'You come from Cuba or Puerto Rico, don't you,' and he answered ill-humoredly—also in English— 'I come from down here.'" Gott continued: "He seemed nervous when he realized we were journalists. When we tried to take his picture he threatened to shoot us with his rifle, and later, when we were allowed to enter the room to see the fallen guerrilla's body, he tried to kick us out."

"There's no doubt the dead man was Commander Guevara," the English reporter said. "I saw him up close. I met the commander three years ago in Havana. It was definitely him. I don't believe that the journalists who arrived the following day were able to identify him with the same certainty I did on Monday afternoon."

A UPI Dispatch

VALLEGRANDE, Bolivia, Oct. 10 (UPI)—I've never seen a dead man who seemed so alive as Ernesto "Che" Guevara.

He didn't look as if he were sleeping because his eyes were open. However, his dead, glassy gaze seemed to fade into eternity.

His pale lips—as pale as paper—offered a smile of sorts, part bitter, part cynical, part ironic. Or was it, perhaps, that he wished to speak?

His head, supported by a board, was raised, giving him the unreal appearance of someone who is alive in death.

His wounds had been cleaned and his body stretched out on a kind of canvas cot placed over a tub in the laundry room of the Señor de Malta hospital.

The tub, which on ordinary days was used to wash the clothes of the patients, had accidentally become the funeral bier of the most famous of the Latin American guerrillas after Fidel Castro.

Everything there was as cold as the corpse.

A water faucet, temporarily silenced. A hose forgotten on the tile floor. Paint chipped away from the brick walls.

The room has no windows and the light, searching for the body, enters through the only door.

2

FIVE YEARS

Alta Grasia January 22, 1933
dear Beatris the surprise is that
I can already swim right on your birth
day I learned to swim
receive kisses from
ERNESTITO

Ana María Guevara de la Serna (sister)

I can't remember him learning how to ride horseback. He was six years older than me; at the time of my earliest memories of him, he already knew how to ride.

Sometimes he rode bareback, other times he rode with a saddle, but without stirrups. Papa wouldn't let us use stirrups because he was afraid we would fall and a foot would get caught. We played "Indians," holding on to the horse by its mane. We lived in the outskirts of the city, in Altagracia, and there was a lot of land around our house.

You could be riding your horse and all of a sudden you'd be rolling on the ground because another kid jumped from a tree and knocked you down. It was also common to gallop along, grab a branch of a tree as you pass under it and hang there while the horse continued alone. The horses were very tame, we'd do with them whatever we wished; so it was easy to learn to ride horseback and you could even stand up on the horse's back. There were never any serious accidents. Falls? Yes, of course.

Editor

I have a photo in front of me. His feet still don't reach the horse's stirrups.

Don Ernesto Guevara Lynch (father)

This photograph was taken on a ranch my mother had in the province of Buenos Aires; he must have been three or four years old. When he grew older he really took a liking to horseback riding. My whole family rode; you'll soon see where my son's enthusiasm for riding came from.

Document

Certificate number three hundred and twenty-four. In the City of Rosario. Department of the same name, Province of Santa Fé, on the fifteenth day of June, nineteen hundred and twenty-eight, at five o'clock in the afternoon, Don Ernesto Rafael Guevara, resident of four hundred and eighty Entre Ríos Street, twenty-four years of age, married, an Argentine citizen, rancher by profession, inhabitant of this City, appeared before me, Ernesto Q. Jimeno, head of the Civil Registry, to declare that in his domicile on the fourteenth day of the current month of June, at five minutes past three in the morning, a white child was born, who is his legitimate son and that of his wife, Doña Celia de la Serna y Llosa, twenty-two years old, Argentine. The aforementioned child is the grandson on the paternal side of Don Roberto Guevara and Doña Ana Linch, and on the maternal side of Don Juan Martín de la Serna and Doña Edelmira Llosa, and he has been given the name Ernesto. All of which has been witnessed by Don Raúl Linch, twenty-two years of age, bachelor, an Argentine citizen, sailor by profession and resident of this City, and Don José Beltrán, thirty years of age, bachelor, citizen of Brazil, driver by profession and residing at two thousand and seventy Catamarla Street.

Having read this record, the witnesses and declarant ratified its contents, signing it along with me.

Don Ernesto

His enthusiasm for horseback riding came not only from the Argentine side of the family but also from the Mexican side, because he also had Mexican blood in him. His paternal great-grandmother, Doña Concepción Castro, was born in Mexico. She and her family lost everything they had in 1848 when the Yankees seized from the Mexicans half of their territory.

My son's great-grandfather, Juan Antonio Guevara, was a pure Argentine gaucho who, under pressure from the dictatorship of General Rosas, had to emigrate to Mexico. He arrived there at the time of the gold rush; at approximately 25 years of age, he was already the leader of the Argentine gold prospectors along the Sacramento River.

The woman who later became my son's great-grandmother lived nearby with her parents. Everyone talked about the group of Argentines and their skill with horses, the lasso and cattle. Stories about them reached the house of Doña Concepción's father, who organized a friendly get-together at his ranch.

The challenge: to see who could rope and turn over a bull the quickest. The winner turned out to be Juan Antonio de Guevara, who later married Doña Concepción; from that marriage came my father, who married Ana Lynch, with whom he later returned to Argentina.

Returning to the child, from the time he was small, my son knew a lot about horses. My father broke horses in, as did my brothers and I. Did he fall a lot? Of course! A horseman has to fall; but he has to pick himself up and mount that horse again. When he was a little older he had a pony with a white spot on its forehead that he rode at my mother's ranch during vacation time.

Ana María

But it wasn't only horses. We also liked to climb trees and scale roofs. That's the way we always were. I have a recollection of the roofs of houses, of treetops, of that iron elevator they used to lift me up in the tall eucalyptuses. They had to try with someone; since I was the smallest they put me inside and raised and lowered me with a rope. The elevator was Ernesto's invention.

We spent a lot of time outdoors and got a lot of exercise. In that period he had already taken up gymnastics. Earlier he couldn't, they didn't let him because he was very ill with asthma. They told Mama he was going to die; only when it seemed as if there were no hope did they let him do whatever he pleased. Up until that time Ernesto had to resign himself to watching other children play, and he looked at them with a very sad face.

The first thing he did was to swim. Papa taught us how to swim in the pool of the Sierras Hotel in Altagracia, which was crowded with people, especially in summer. There were some very large parks there; we played there so often we knew the place perfectly.

Don Ernesto

His asthma began very early. One day he got a fever and the doctor said it wasn't serious; a heavy flu, he said. Then there were complications: pneumonia. In May 1930, he came down with the asthma that would follow him throughout life. We moved to the capital because of the air; then to Alto de Paraná, in Misiones. No kind of climate suited him though. We picked up our things and returned to the capital. From there we went to Córdova and finally to Altagracia. Each time we tried to return home, his attacks grew worse. It would break my heart because the first thing he would stammer was "Injection, Papito."

Ana Mariá

We lived in several different houses in Altagracia. One house we rented was called Villa Chichita. It had two floors and a gable roof, very similar to houses they have in southern Italy. It had a lot of rooms and a real family, work, school atmosphere.

In the winter we sat by the fireplace. Each person did what he or she wanted. Some preferred conversation, others playing table games or reading. Ernesto loved poetry, and when we would get together he would begin reciting and we would follow suit. One person would read a poem and another would follow. Music, no; he had no musical skills.

Like Roberto, he learned how to read at home. Mama taught them. They learned to read quickly and very well. He didn't leave the house in that period, and he read a lot. He read Salgari, Jules Verne, Jack London and other authors I can't remember. Then he took on Alexandre Dumas. When he began school, they started him in second grade.

Don Ernesto

Everyone in the family read a lot, but particularly Ernesto. He leaned toward the Spanish classics, and his favorite book at the time was *Quixote*. He somehow managed to get hold of the books of Blasco Ibáñez and Pérez Galdós. Later he read León Felipe.

Forgive me for jumping around in his childhood. For example, when he was barely four years old he wrote to his aunt Beatriz, tracing the letters with his mother's hand over his and signing "TT," or Teté, the affectionate nickname he later used as a pseudonym to write to us, outwitting the intelligence agencies. We were the only ones who knew him by that name.

Anecdotes, anecdotes... There's an anecdote for every day. Don't forget he was the leader of a gang of more than twenty boys. There was a meadow in back of the house I never went to. Ernesto and his friends built four rows of trenches there and linked them with tunnels. They would divide themselves into two factions and the battle would begin. Their weapons were taken from nature: stones, which they would shoot with slings. Everything would have continued as it was had not one of the boys been hurt in one of the battles and run away. When they saw me arrive on the scene, they all took off.

It was the time of the Spanish civil war. Ernesto followed developments very closely on a map. He and his friends reenacted the battles. They would go out into the hills to train. They walked long distances, as if they were guerrillas.

Near the house was an empty lot where a ram was left to graze. The children were afraid of it, but Ernesto went to meet it head-on.

The animal saw him coming and lowered its head, showing its unfriendly horns. The child gauged the terrain. He was determined, though he felt weak in the knees. The animal charged and the child sidestepped him. The scene was repeated over and over again until Ernesto managed to grab hold of its horns. Excited, the other boys drew closer; the bullring shrank in size.

The animal and the child fell to the ground. One of them had to give in. The animal tried to free itself from the grasp that bound it; Ernesto tried to reduce the ram to obedience. Gradually one of them surrendered: the ram.

The child brushed himself off and fixed his gaze on the loser. His friends patted him on the back. He went to the center ring; his short pants exposed bare knees that had been scratched in the skirmish. His chest heaved up and down. Did he drop his inhaler? His hands, impatient, searched his pockets.

His First Shot

Dear Beatriz:
Why don't you come
to visit us? The canary sings
all day long
I have a bunch of friends with
whom we always play
There are about 15 of them One has a
rifle I don't have asthma
but I take an elixir every
night Give lots of kisses to
grandma and a big hug from
ERNESTITO

Five Years

Don Ernesto

At the time we lived in Altagracia, I had a .38-caliber, long-barreled revolver. Ernesto was about eight years old and he liked to watch me shoot. He would stack up a few bricks at a given distance, and I would shoot at them.

You should have seen his face when the bricks would break into pieces. First they would split in two, then four, and so on until finally they crumbled into fragments.

One day I handed him the revolver. He looked at it and then at the target. I showed him how to position himself and take aim, to fill his lungs with air and as he exhaled little by little to slowly pull the trigger. The sound of the gun firing surprised him, and the bullet went wide of the target.

Shortly after the victory of the Cuban Revolution, we were together in El Pedrero, near his headquarters in Escambray. My son was carrying a Belgian pistol on his waist, and I had an Argentine Colt 45.

"Shall we shoot?" he asked. We chose a tree as our target. All his *compañeros* gathered around. He drew his pistol from its sheath and slowly took aim. As he pulled the trigger, I heard a heavy burst of gunfire. I was astounded. I looked around and realized that his *compañeros* had fired along with him. The tree trunk was full of bullet holes. As he replaced his gun he looked at me, smiling. There was no need for me to shoot. For a second I recalled that day in Altagracia.

Ana Mariá

He was fond of us all. Celia and he were perhaps the closest, although sometimes they fought like a cat and dog. He liked playing with Roberto best. He was very protective of me. Ours wasn't a relationship of equals; he acted toward me as one would expect an older brother to, and not very respectfully at that. His friends? The people of the *barrio*, the children of the poor families.

I should point out that he had two kinds of friends: those that came to spend the summer, from petit-bourgeois families; and the poor. He felt more comfortable with the latter; they went on outings together.

Because of his disposition, he was obviously quite different culturally from the other children, and he quickly stood out. It wasn't that he liked to order the others around; he didn't. But when everyone gave their opinion about something and he gave his, everyone all of a sudden agreed with him.

One time Papa bought a motorcycle (which, for sure, didn't last very long), and my brother wanted to start it. He tried and tried but nothing happened. So he stuck his fingers in his mouth and whistled, and kids appeared from all directions. About ten of them came. They all pitched in until they finally started it. That was the way it was because he never failed his friends either. I felt very good being with him; it was as if he would fill up your life.

Our childhood was beautiful. When we lived in Villa Nidia we were always playing, running, making up games. One time Ernesto was balancing on a tree where we used to hang hammocks, and he fell. Lying there on the ground, he looked like he was dead. I went toward him, frightened, and suddenly he jumped to his feet in front of me.

Asthma always affected him when he was playing games. He was even allergic to some trees. My parents didn't know what to do to help him. They were always looking for any kind of medicine that might give him some relief. Beatriz, my aunt in Buenos Aires, joined the search. She sent him tubes of Yanal cream, an antiasthmatic remedy that had stirred some interest. And since you can't lose by trying, Ernesto also began to smoke.

Yes, when he was four or five years old, in Altagracia, he began to smoke. Not normal cigarettes, but Dr. Andreu's antiasthmatic cigarettes which were very smelly. Smoking as a small child, he attracted a lot of attention from people.

Doña Celia de la Serna de Guevara (mother)

I received a notice from the Ministry of Education saying that my son, who was seven years old, hadn't registered at any elementary institution of learning. I answered immediately. Since Ernesto couldn't go to school because of his asthma, I had taught him how to read and write. He attended only second and third grades regularly; in fourth, fifth and sixth grades he went to school when he could. His brothers would copy down his schoolwork and he would study at home.

Ana María

Mama's car was very old. I don't know why we called it the "Catramina"; that name, for me, is synonymous with something very old. It was a coupe, with one of those covers that you raise from the back and two seats with a canvas roof appear. Every morning, trying to start it, the show would begin. You had to crank it, and they [Mama and the children] could almost never start it. We would call Papa to get it to work.

Oviedo Zelaya (Ernesto's first teacher in Altagracia)

I remember his mother, Doña Celia. She was very beautiful. She wore her hair with buns on both sides. I believe she was the first woman I ever saw wearing long pants. She was a very resolute woman. She had an old car that she fixed herself when she needed to. She would get down on the ground and look for what was wrong with it. And this happened frequently, because the car was always packed with children, both her own and other people's. She was very democratic, very open.

José Aguilar* (childhood friend)

I remember the teacher was in the habit of spanking the children, and for some reason or another she was going to spank Ernesto. He caused quite a ruckus because he had a brick in the seat of his trousers and when she hit him . . .

*The Aguilar family arrived in Argentina from Spain. That is, the mother and children came; the father stayed in one of Franco's prisons. The children were afflicted by the war. The family became close to the Guevaras.

José Aguilar

Doña Celia taught him French, and he began reading Baudelaire. He also read Spanish poetry. I remember him repeating these lines: "it was a lie / a lie / that had become the sad truth /that his steps could be heard / in Madrid, which no longer exists."

An Initial Conclusion

Editor

In school, Ernesto became close friends with a boy his age, Tomás Granados. They talked between classes, went to parties together. At that time, the university students were restive. They acted quickly, going out on strike. The police intervened and some were beaten and detained. Tomas's brother Alberto was arrested. The food in jail was terrible, so Tomas took food to his older brother, and Ernesto accompanied him. During one of the visits, Alberto suggested that the high school students take to the streets so that people in the city would learn that the university students have been imprisoned without trial.

Ernesto listened to him attentively and finally commented: "You've got to be kidding, Alberto! Take to the streets and let the police chase us away with clubs? No way. I'll only go out if they give me a revolver."

Alberto listened to him, astonished. What is this kid saying? It was a prelude to a friendship that would last for years. Ernesto was in his second year of high school; Alberto, his second year of medical school.

Alberto Granados

We called him "Pelao" ["Baldy"] because he wore his hair cut very short. We all had several nicknames, but that was the one that stuck to him the most. He and I had special names for each other. He called me "Mial" and I called him "Fuser." My grandmother always called me "Mi Alberto," so that's where he got Mial. As far as Fuser goes, when we played soccer and were losing, he would come running and say to me, "Move it, let's get going, 'cause here comes the furibundo [furious] Serna!" And Fuser came from putting together the first syllables of furibundo and Serna [his mother's family name].

When it came to chess, he had lots of friends: Tomás, Calica Ferrer, me and even an uncle of mine. We would watch our kings be dethroned, succumbing to his quick moves leading to checkmate. He had a tendency to lose pieces in order to gain an advantageous position.

We would go to the movies. He liked the Italian directors and [Henry] Fonda's acting in *The Grapes of Wrath*. He enjoyed watching James Stewart and [Edward G.] Robinson. Of the Argentines, he liked Petrony, the character actor, best, and in theater his favorite was Narciso Ibáñez. He also loved westerns, because of the action.

Elio G. Constantin (Cuban journalist)

After waiting a while at the School of Medicine in Buenos Aires, they brought us the records of Ernesto Guevara, number 59 395.

The records indicate that he entered the school in December 1947, at 19 years of age. He graduated on April 11, 1953, just a few months before the attack on the Moncada barracks.

The extracurricular activities mentioned in the records include sports and cultural activities. For example, on June 30, 1949, he signed up for the chess and rugby programs, playing in the latter as a scrum-half. It also said that he drew, painted and was interested in artistic photography, and that he took an enthusiastic interest in literature.

A year later, his sporting credentials, in addition to rugby and chess, included swimming and soccer. He was a member of the Atalaya Rugby Club, but changed his position to fullback.

Curiously, something is missing from the records of medical student Ernesto Guevara de la Serna: his portrait, undoubtedly removed out of popular devotion. Another piece of information:

He participated in the first University Olympics, held in 1948, when he was 20 years old. He took part in the chess tournament and in track and field, clearing 2.8 meters in the pole vault competition. The winners of the contest were not recorded.

Editor

Studying medicine was not originally part of his plans. Ernesto passed the entrance exams for engineering school. Many of his friends thought he'd choose mathematics, because of his skill in the subject; others thought he'd be a physics or a chemistry major, or something of that sort.

His paternal grandmother was taken ill and her health worsened. Her inevitable death came after fifteen days of fruitless efforts. Ernesto helped take care of her and it was around this time that he first decided to study medicine.

José Aguilar

Ernesto got a six-hour-a-day job in the Buenos Aires city government. He also did volunteer work with the Institute for the Investigation of Allergies. At the time he was writing a dictionary of philosophy for his personal use, and he worked on it at the office. By coincidence, this won him a promotion, because his supervisor came to the office at a time when everyone was supposed to be there, and he found only Ernesto. He congratulated Ernesto for being so responsible; little did he know that Ernesto was doing something completely unrelated to his job.

Don Ernesto

Ernesto only had three subjects left to graduate from the university, but instead of staying in the city to study he decided to travel to San Francisco de Altagracia to a leprosarium where Alberto worked. The distance: 1,600 kilometers. The means of transportation: a bicycle with a small Cucciolo motor. He took everything he needed except for money: a cap and dark glasses, a thick overcoat for the cold, a spare tire slung crosswise over his shoulder and chest, and a gasoline can tied to his waist. He crossed the province of Santa Fe, the north of Córdova and the eastern part of Mendoza. Along the way he studied.

Alberto Granados

He told me about the way he traveled. He would hit the road very early, taking advantage of the cool weather, and around ten or eleven o'clock, when the sun heated up the pavement, he would search for the shade and turn to his books. Often a truck would stop. "Hey kid, do you want a ride?" "No. I have forty-five minutes left," he would answer, and continue studying.

So he came to the leprosarium and toured the different facilities. There they fixed his bicycle, which was in bad shape. His marks that year weren't high, but he passed his courses, and what he did study, he studied thoroughly.

Ana María

He liked to meet people. When he went on a trip he would stop at farms and quickly make friends. He would eat with the *campesinos* and farmhands and enjoyed listening to them. Sometimes, even though he had a relative nearby, he would stay in the houses of people who invited him to spend the night. He preferred making new friends.

He made good friends, very good friends—or big enemies. He was very cutting, incisive, ironic. It's a trait of the de la Serna family. He perceived things intuitively and got down to the bottom of them.

Alberto Granados

I've always said that you can hate Pelao or you can love him, but you can't be indifferent. He says what he feels regardless of others' opinions, and if he doesn't want to hurt someone, he keeps quiet. He shuns protocol and is reluctant to wear a jacket and tie.

3

TWO PROFESSIONALS WASTE THEIR TIME

Palenque

There is something still living in your stone,
sister of the green dawns.
Your silence of ancestral spirits
scandalizes the royal tombs.

The indifferent pickax
of a know-it-all with boring spectacles
wounds you in the heart
and the insolent affront
of an idiot, oh! of a gringo tourist
slaps you in the face.
But you have something that is alive.

I don't know what it is;
the jungle gives you an offering, an embrace of trunks
and even the tangled mercy of its roots.
A huge zoologist displays the pin
with which he will secure your temples to a trunk
and still you do not die.

What force sustains you
beyond the passing of centuries,
living and throbbing as in your youth?
What god, at the end of a long day,
blows a life-giving breeze on your stelae?

Is it the cheerful sun of the tropics?
Why would it not do the same in Chichén-Itzá?
Is it the amiable embrace of the forest
or the melodious song of the birds?
Why then does Quiriguá sleep more deeply?
Is it the music of the sonorous spring
rushing through the crags of the sierra?
The Incas have died, notwithstanding.

—Ernesto

Editor

More months of studying and classrooms. He plunged into some subjects with enthusiasm; others he passed because he had to. It was September 1950, and after sending notice, he decided to visit Córdova again. He knew nothing about the conversation held by his friends the Granados brothers, Tomás and Alberto (who had left his position in the leprosarium). Alberto wanted to take a trip around South America; Tomás quickly found his brother a traveling companion: Ernesto.

Alberto didn't really have to be convinced. For quite a while both he and Ernesto had thought about the possibility of traveling together. Ernesto told Alberto he could count on him, but that he'd have to wait until he passed a few exams. They set a December departure date and prepared to leave.

Their families reacted to their plans quickly and vociferously. What madness! Two professionals wasting their time traveling around! They repaired, as well as they could, the Norton 500, model 39 motorbike they chose to rove around the continent on. How will they work it out if only Alberto has an international driver's license? Granados will drive in the cities, they decide, and his friend will drive on the highways.

The twenty-fifth of December arrived. They took care of last minute details. Each one of them had a traveling bag for the things they'd need on the trip. Alberto was in charge of this end of the preparations and made two lists, one for himself and one for his friend. Ernesto's list read:

Bag, Second in Command (Fuser)

1 pair of swimming trucks	1 knife
1 pair of gloves	1 fork
2 pullovers	1 spoon
2 pairs of pants	1 dish
1 pair of long johns	1 aluminum cup
1 undershirt	1 spoon [sic]
2 pairs of synthetic underpants	1 scarf
4 shirts	1 [illegible]
2 pairs of woolen socks	1 turtleneck sweater
2 pairs of nylon socks	1 pair of slippers

In addition, they took two portable cots, a sleeping bag made by Granados, some tools, a tent and even two old Smith & Wesson revolvers.

At the Granados house, the family went outside to bid them farewell. It was not inconceivable that the motorcycle would be as stubborn as a mule and refuse to move forward, so heavy was its load. They rode down the streets of Córdova. They arrived at an intersection, and the light turned red at the same moment that Ernesto, with a sudden movement, looked backward. They barely missed colliding with a passing streetcar. The passengers shouted insults at them. Their baggage almost slid off.

"Hey, stop!" ordered Ernesto. Alberto pretended not to hear him and continued some two hundred meters forward.

"Why didn't you stop? What an imbecile you are! Didn't you see that our baggage almost fell off?"

"Didn't you see that my family was still outside the house?" Alberto responded. "If I had stopped after we almost crashed, they would have been at us about the trip again."

They had handled their first mishap well enough. When they arrived in Buenos Aires, part of Ernesto's family reprimanded them, but Celia, his mother, agreed with their plans and encouraged them, although she made her son promise that he would return in time to take his remaining exams at the university.

They spent New Year's Eve in Ernesto's house at 2180 Arao St. and left on the first, traveling toward the southern part of Argentina in order to avoid the steep Andean mountains in the north. Chile was their next destination. They also had a new traveling companion: "Come Back," a German shepherd puppy Ernesto was bringing as a gift to his girlfriend, who was in Miramar.

The route they chose wasn't exactly the most appropriate to their means of transportation. Even though they expected to climb mountain roads and pass by sheer cliffs, they were nevertheless surprised when the wheels of the motorbike began to constantly skid on the sand covering the southern roads. They continued forward, frequently falling. On one occasion they counted fourteen spills in a one-kilometer stretch.

As they traveled along, they questioned, inquired. They copied the name of each town they visited in their diaries. One of their stops lasted longer than they expected: "Come Back" disappeared, and they didn't want to abandon him. They searched the area, but he seemed to have vanished into thin air. Just as they had gotten on their motorcycle and were about to leave, they heard the puppy's cry, picked him up and continued on their journey.

Miramar was within sight. There the travelers found human warmth that compensated for the punishing cold of the road. "Come Back" passed from one set of hands to another until he was given to Chichina. Ernesto's sister Ana María was also there; there was no need to set up the tent; they slept in the house.

They relaxed, went out, had a good time; they also used the time to work on the motorbike. During a conversation one night, Ernesto gave his opinion about the nationalization of health care in Great Britain.

Low on money, Ernesto and Alberto decided to go to a casino. Each of them risked a few pesos at the roulette wheel. Ernesto played red and the ball ended up on black. Over and over again the fickle roulette ball played tricks with him, and he lost his bets. "Listen, Pelao," his friend finally said to him, "I figure we've already lost around 10 kilometers' worth of gasoline. No more!"

Plenty of jokes about the trip were made; here, too, their friends and family, although young, were skeptical. Even if the trip had ended at that point, however, it could hardly have been considered lost time.

A week had passed since they arrived in Miramar. The motorcycle sounded like new. The road beckoned. At times, when they hit a pothole, the motorbike reared up on its back wheel like a colt.

Further and further from Buenos Aires they went, but were nevertheless determined to continue. There was a writer—Ciro Alegría is his name—who taught them, unintentionally, that America can be the first link in getting to know the world. The trip in and of itself was an adventure; but adventures can take one on very different paths. These travelers were not seeking material wealth, personal success or, much less, violence. Although they didn't announce it to the world, nor were they particularly conscious of it at the time, they were led by a social awareness, which would bear fruit later.

They had read about the penetration of U.S. corporations and consortiums throughout America, about exploitation. But this occurred in a more covert form in Argentina; they wished to see it with their own eyes.

On the coast is Argentina's "Switzerland." There are many lakes and few poor people there. The houses are well-built, comfortable. The prices and opulence are a red light for those on the bottom and a green light for an elite. The landscape, with its luxuriant forests and high-altitude lakes, is impressive. It is a rugged and wild habitat. By chance they met an acquaintance from Miramar, who told them that an auto show would be held there soon. The travelers decided to stay on for a while.

The smell of meat roasting on the grill was in the air. Ernesto and his friend approached the owner of the stand and asked him if he needed helpers; he told them he did. In this way they were fed and made a little money.

Chile wasn't far away. The mountain range rose majestically, its height a constant challenge they couldn't ignore. Heading uphill, the motorcycle sputtered. Morning had just passed and they had decided to rest a while, when they came upon a lake that drew their attention. They turned several meters off the road to set up camp.

The late afternoon sun slipped from the sky. Branches crackled in the improvised campfire. The water in the kettle was boiling, and Ernesto added the maté. The air was somewhat chilly, and they hadn't removed their jackets. Someone approached. The stranger greeted them and they returned the greeting. Granados and the newcomer struck up a conversation.

"Traveling?" the stranger asked. "Yes, we're traveling," Alberto responded. "Are you from around here?"

The stranger hesitated before answering. His eyes passed over their belongings, pausing when they reach the Norton.

"That's a pretty fine bike, eh? It must have cost you a bundle, no?"

"A bit, my man, a bit."

Ernesto calmly joined them, and with the kettle in his hand, he poured a gourd of maté. Facing the man, who was now looking at one of their bags, he said, "Have a maté, brother?" The man accepted the maté and took a long sip through the metal straw. His eyes closed halfway; he appeared to enjoy the bitter brew.

"Did you know there's a Chilean thief around here who steals things from travelers?" he said. "Really?" answered Granados, more as an invitation to continue the conversation than an indication of surprise.

The man took another sip of maté. Ernesto, sitting on the ground off to one side, was absently gazing toward the lake.

"Your jackets are practically new: anyone could get a good price for them," the man said to Alberto. "And do you know this area well?" Alberto asked. The man let out a sly laugh and nodded his head. "Is the border nearby?" "Just over there," said the man, pointing indifferently. "Are you going to spend the night here?" he added. "Do you think we should?" countered Granados.

The man scratched his head as if he were thinking, and then said, "And you're not afraid of being robbed? Listen, you..."

An explosion, which because of the prevailing calm seemed like the boom of a small cannon, almost lifted them off the ground. The man looked around with his eyes wide open. Ernesto was holding the Smith & Wesson, which he had drawn from under his right pant leg just a moment before. A flock of ducks took flight over the lake; one of them still floated on the water, cut down by the bullet.

"Alberto, look," Ernesto called. "Did you see how I got him?"

The man didn't even wait to say goodbye; he was a blurred figure on the road. The two friends looked at each other. Ernesto laughed his asthmatic laugh.

The next morning they reach the border, by a lake the Argentines call Nahuelhuapi and the Chileans call Lago de Todos los Santos (All Saints' Lake). In the distance they see a volcano, its slopes wrapped in a dress of lava that formed gradually as a result of eruptions and the passing of centuries of time. They are in Chile. It has taken them thirty days since their departure from Buenos Aires to cross the continent. The trip is a reality.

It doesn't occur to anyone who sees them that they have come from so far away or that they will get much further, especially now that inclines are a constant factor. They are happy to smell the breeze of the Pacific Ocean. For Alberto it will be his first encounter with the sea. For his friend, though he is accustomed to the waters of the Atlantic at Mar del Plata, the experience is no less interesting. They recover their strength, and mix with people in the port of Osorno.

Their next stop is the town of Temuco, where social contrasts open up before them, as they will throughout the remainder of their journey. More important than the landscape are the people, how they live, how they are exploited. The gulf between the powerful and the dispossessed is obvious; they see it, touch it first-hand. On the other hand, there is their scientific interest. The two young men meet a journalist, who turns them into news; they appear in the local newspaper, posing for the photographer.

TWO ARGENTINIAN LEPROSY EXPERTS TOUR SOUTH AMERICA ON A MOTORBIKE

Two Argentinian medical experts who are traveling around South America on a motorcycle arrived in Temuco yesterday.

Alberto Granados, doctor of biochemistry, and Ernesto Guevara Serna, medical student at the University of Buenos Aires, left the province of Córdova on December 29 on a journey they hope will bring them to the principal countries of South America. After passing through northern Argentina, they entered Chile at Peulla, and then visited Petrobué, Osorno and Valdivia. Yesterday they traveled on their motorcycle from Valdivia to Temuco.

LEPROSY SPECIALISTS

The visiting scientists specialize in the treatment of leprosy and other illnesses derived from this terrible disease. They have a broad knowledge of the leprosy problem as it affects their country, and they themselves treat approximately 3,000 patients at the Cerritos, Diamantes, General Rodríguez, Córdova and Posadas leprosariums.

They have also visited institutions for treating this disease in Brazil, one of the countries with a high percentage of leprosy victims.

INTEREST IN EASTER ISLAND
In addition to their interest in learning about health conditions in different South American countries, Granados and Guevara—who are paying for the trip out of their own pockets—are particularly interested in seeing the Chilean leprosarium of Rapa Nui. In Valparaíso, the visiting medical experts intend to contact the directors of the Society of Friends of Easter Island to inquire about the possibility of visiting that remote leprosarium on the Chilean island in the Pacific.

The traveler-scientists expect to end their tour in Venezuela. After having spent a day in Temuco, Granados and Guevara will leave for Concepción.

Accident

Ernesto was driving the motorbike. They were having a lively conversation, although the wind carried many of their words away. For several days now the hand brake hadn't been working. Heading downhill, the bike gathered excessive speed. Ernesto tried to slow their descent with the foot brake; he applied it several times, but it didn't respond.

The choices were not exactly auspicious. At their right was a seemingly bottomless precipice. At their left, a rock cliff jutted out with its silent threat of violence. Ahead there was a bridge—which would have been a great help to them were not an approaching herd of cattle blocking their path. They only had a few seconds to act.

"Runt, the brakes are broken," Ernesto said. "Yes, they're broken," said Granados, as he tried to figure out what they could do. He came up with something.

"Listen Pelao, put it in second gear, then in first, and run the motorbike into the cliff. But remember, jump off before it hits!"

Pelao squeezed down into his seat and began to follow his friend's instructions. He put it in second gear; the wall approached. As he was about to put it into first, he felt for a split-second that part of their load had fallen off. There was no time to look back; he couldn't see that Alberto had jumped off and become entangled in the baggy trousers he was wearing.

First gear. Five, three, two meters: the cliff. Ernesto jumps, the bike hits the cliff and it lets out a moan, a sort of hoarse-sounding lament. Granados gets up, still not feeling his bruises. He goes to the motorcycle and turns off the motor to avoid the possibility of it catching on fire.

The two friends look at each other instinctively, and then their eyes turn toward the motorbike. A dead calm takes hold. The only sound heard is the occasional mooing of cattle in the distance. On their right is the abyss. A few drops of oil fall and mix with the dust of the road. The cover on the motor has cracked. Somehow they managed to straggle in to the nearest town.

The cost of repairing the motorcycle will considerably diminish their funds. From a roadside handbill they learn they've arrived in Los Angeles. People look at them with curiosity. They move slowly, losing oil along the way.

As Usual, Taking the Most Difficult Path

It's midday when they arrive in town. Los Angeles is a pretty place, surrounded by woods. Accustomed to making friends easily, they meet a young woman who, though no great beauty, attracts them with her personable manner. The girl is interested in the travelers; they tell her their story.

Since they have no place to sleep, she suggests they go to the fire station, where her father is chief of the all-volunteer force.

The two fire engines take up most of the space at the station. Ernesto settles down for the night without much fuss; Alberto climbs a spiral staircase and picks a spot that has been smoothed out by passing footsteps. Exhausted, they immediately fall asleep.

Granados hears a deafening roar, as if one hundred black-smiths were all pounding a giant anvil at the same time. His head feels like it's going to explode. Is it, perhaps, the roof caving in? Am I dreaming? he thinks. In the midst of his lethargy, he begins to discern a single word.

Below, Ernesto hastily shakes off his drowsiness; he senses a bell rousing him from his sleep and manages to catch the word on everyone's lips: fire!

A throng of volunteer fire fighters burst into the station, each taking up his place. The sirens wail; the fire engines split the calm of the night.

The beams of the wooden ship crackle, and the flames endeavor to swallow the darkness. The wind stirs up a cloud of ashes. The tension runs as strong as the streams of water spurting from the hoses. The fire fighters split into two groups. Alberto goes with the group carrying the water hoses, and "Pelao," according to Alberto, "as usual, went where things seemed most difficult to him."

Years later, recalling the fire and his friend's role, Granados would comment: "The fire was extinguished and he returned, very pleased, with a pair of kittens he had saved. He was extremely proud. They treated us like heroes and gave us two small flags in honor of our 'exploit.'"

They arrived as strangers and leave as friends. The motorbike isn't exactly in the best of shape. The chief of the volunteer fire fighters speaks with a truck driver who often makes trips to the Chilean capital, and asks him to give the two a lift.

The driver has an unfriendly face and constantly cracks jokes. He doesn't pass up the chance to tell Ernesto and his friend that they are "weaklings" from the city.

Offended, Ernesto is determined to respond to the challenge. His opportunity soon arrives.

The truck stops and the driver negotiates a price for hauling some wardrobes. Summoning "his nervous energy," as his friend calls it, Ernesto lifts one of the heavy pieces of furniture onto the truck by himself. Then he blurts out to the driver, "Now let's see where you put the rest of them."

The man looks at him; Ernesto's feat has won his respect.

When they arrive in Santiago de Chile, they look up an Argentine acquaintance, an auto salesman, and ask him for a place to leave the second and most important casualty of the ride: the Norton, model 39.

On Foot

The motorbike sits silent and alone in a corner. It will soon be devoured by rust. It has helped bring them to the reality of the men and women of the continent. Though they have some first-hand information, they're not satisfied; they need more. Behind them is a road traveled, but ahead there remains much more. They want to see the nitrate and copper regions of Chile; to fill themselves with the image of those faces dried-out by so much hunger and frustration. They plan to visit Chuquicamata, where, they've heard, there are men who day after day wear themselves out in silence. Having decided to go there from Valparaíso, they ask around and find a fruit-hauling truck that's going in their direction. They speak to the driver and offer to work as his assistants.

The truck is empty when they leave, but on the way they pick up a load of grapes. They have worked hard, and the grapes stimulate their appetite in such a way that they never feel satisfied. They arrived in Valparaíso full, very full.

They've heard there is an organization in this port city called the Friends of Easter Island, and have been planning to visit the leprosarium there. It won't be easy; they've been told that a boat goes there only once every six months.

At night, the docks are a temptation. The boats rest in the calm nocturnal waters of the port. The two friends wonder what course to take and decide to board one of the anchored boats and hide in the lavatory. They are stowaways.

Among the many horn blasts they hear in the port, one seems more powerful than the rest. The boat they have chosen signals it is going out to sea. The motors broadcast the ship's movement, and the crew rushes around.

From their hiding place they hear footsteps approaching. Suddenly the bathroom door is thrown open.

"Hey, what are you lazy bums doing there? Do you want me to throw you into the sea?" The voice is laden with threats. "Let's see then, let's go to the captain."

The introduction takes place in less than ideal circumstances, but they do manage to explain who they are and the reason for their journey. As usual, they offer to do whatever job is requested of them. The captain, sparing in his use of words, allows them to remain on board. Alberto works as a cook's helper; Ernesto has worse luck: His task is to clean the lavatories. Behind them, the coastline recedes in the distance.

One afternoon they strike up a conversation with the captain. He's curious about their life in Argentina, and the two young men speak with him in great detail, even showing him the newspaper clipping from Temuco. The captain listens to them silently; only when they finish, as if to stave off the loneliness of the ocean, he asks, "Do you know how to play canasta?" "Of course!" Granados immediately reponds. "Who doesn't?"

Night falls. In the captain's cabin there's an uncustomary sense of excitement. The cards pass from hand to hand. Formalities are dispensed with; a rapport is established. The captain stops the game and calls. "Hey, cook!" The cook comes immediately and listens to the order: "Bring omelets for everybody."

The captain deals the cards. The cook, confused, hasn't budged. The almost imperceptible sound of the cards falling on the table stops. The cook senses his boss is watching him; resentful of the violation of the ship's hierarchy, he chides the captain in a tone of disgust.

"But captain, first..." Under the captains gaze, he wavers. "First I would have to take my assistants along."

"Listen. If these gentlemen hadn't come on board you wouldn't have any assistants." The captain pulls an ace of spades from his hand. "In other words, stop screwing around and bring the omelets!"

The two friends don't say a word, but they exchange a fleeting glance. The word "gentlemen" seems amusing and strange to them. So they are no longer stowaways, but two gentlemen who boarded the ship. The look on the cook's face is understandable; Alberto knows he'll have a hard time if he's still under the cook's command the following day. Days later he would find the map they used to plot their trip floating in a bucket of water.

Now they are guests on the ship, and the captain constantly summons them: "Forget about working! Come here and tell me somethiing about Buenos Aires, about Chile. How are things there?"

Alberto carries on in a grand manner, and the captain listens. Ernesto is tight-lipped, although he enjoys the conversation. They even take some pictures. At a port of call, the captain proves his sincerity. Upon arriving at the port, they receive a visit from customs agents. "Come over here," the captain urges them. He opens a door, and once they are inside, he locks it shut. "You are in my cabin; no one will think of looking for you here."

When it's time to say goodbye, the captain invites them to dinner. They break open a few bottles. Alberto savors the flavor of the drink; Ernesto drinks a small amount, out of courtesy. They have a new friend, but they've gone beyond their projected point of disembarkation. They are in Antofagasta.

Attempting to take advantage of what the place has to offer, they head for the nitrate mines. The area has decayed quite a bit. The residents tell them that it has been in decline since the end of World War II. The desert surrounds them. During the day, the heat scorches them; at night, the cold is penetrating. They try to make their way to Chuquicamata.

A Harsh Reality

It takes a lot of sweat and hard work to dig the copper from the mine. The miners and their families wear the grimace of misery on their faces. The copper is Chile's, but it doesn't belong to the Chileans. The Braden Copper Company is the lord and master of the area.

According to Granados, a highly-educated technician earns the equivalent of one hundred dollars a month, while the "mister's" driver—who doubles as a bodyguard—earns four hundred.

It has become very difficult for the unions to organize workers. At times they encounter open repression; other times the measures taken against them are more subtle, though no less repugnant. When they call a mass meeting, the owner's driver appears on the scene to nobly announce that the party is on him that night, that he'll order the brothel to be closed so the miners can drink and make merry for free. In this way he can effectively block the union's organizing efforts and save the company's skin for the mere sum of forty-five dollars.

They also try to undermine the workers' class consciousness. Some more qualified workers are given prefabricated houses, while the great majority of miners live in tin shacks—an abysmal difference.

"We also took note of the company's tricks," Granados said. "Imagine, they would make a concentrated solution out of the ore and appraise its mineral content. I don't remember the exact figure they set, but let's say it was 12 percent. If the ore had 14 percent mineral, they said fine, and paid twelve. And a tax had to be paid on that too. So they paid twelve. But if they said it had 11.8, they stopped right there and shut off the tap because it was two-tenths short.

"We saw all kinds of things there in the copper mines. We talked with people from company headquarters and had a rather unpleasant interview with the manager, who made us wait for several hours before giving us permission to visit the mines."

The two friends stay overnight in Chuquicamata. They improvise a bedroom in the sentry booth used by the mine's private police. Upon waking, Granados is confronted with an image he would later remember vividly.

"Pelao was lying with his head right next to the boot of the owner's henchman. It was an unpleasant image that stayed in my mind, and as the years passed by and Pelao was no longer Pelao, well, that image would come back to me and I'd think, with one quick stamp of his foot he could have done him in. I sure didn't like the sight of Pelao at the feet of a military man!"

Below One Can See the Condors Fly

Seen from below, the truck in which they were traveling looked like a tiny dot. The altiplano is so high, they are having trouble breathing. In the valley one can see the condors fly. The travelers are heading toward Peru. Soon they will arrive in Machu Picchu, a place they have wanted to visit for a long time.

They are traveling the same route taken over four hundred years ago by Almagro and Valdivia in their conquest of Chile. They can imagine how hard the trip was for those men with their heavy garments and weapons. Granados makes an occasional comment; his friend travels in silence. They'll remember the scenery for as long as they are alive. Breaking the shell of silence that has enveloped them, the driver tells them they will arrive shortly in Tacna. They pick up their belongings, say goodbye and head off in another direction, toward the highest lake in the world, Lake Titicaca, at 3,815 meters above sea level.

Here they also touch human misery, and not without feeling the pain themselves. They are traveling in the back of an open truck. The cold permeates their bones. It begins to rain. The truck winds around dangerous curves. The landscape takes on a secondary importance. The two friends focus their attention on an Indian woman riding with them. Judging by her wrinkled face and thin body, she is more than eighty years old. Her body bent over, she is obviously suffering from the cold and rain. The two look at each other, not knowing what to do, and the voice of the truck driver soon rings out, "Have those two Argentines get out and come up front to the cabin with me."

"Why not have the old woman go inside? We can take the rain," Granados suggests. The driver's response cuts through the dampness. "I don't let Indians in my cabin."

The words are spoken as if they were something routine, very natural. To the driver's surprise, Granados ends the discussion abruptly. "You go on then. We're staying here."

Later they'll witness even crueler incidents. The Indians' passivity seems extraordinary to them. A white man or a person of mixed race can take an Indian's seat from him, or push Indians over in order to be more comfortable. It is a result of centuries of exploitation. Ernesto observes it all. He listens. He learns.

They manage to get hold of a straw raft; on it, they ride around Lake Titicaca. They're anxious to leave for Cuzco, the distant city where Tupac Amaru was cut into pieces.

From Cuzco to Machu Picchu

Ernesto and Granados visit the largest fortress of the Incan empire. They walk through Sascsahuamán, touching the stones and seeing for themselves how much beautiful, detailed work these inhabitants of America created before the arrival of the Spanish colonizers. They discover the Inca library and adopt it as their general headquarters. Absorbed in the wealth of books there, they become oblivious to their surroundings, barely noticing the people looking at them with a combination of curiosity and resentment, as if they were beings from another planet.

Alberto decides to visit an acquaintance of his, a doctor who lives in the city. They knock on the door; when it opens, there are no handshakes, nor words of welcome. Alberto identifies himself, but his acquaintance doesn't recognize him behind his dirty clothes and unkempt beard.

He persists, telling him to try to remember, reminding him they met several years earlier at a conference. Things are going poorly, until a photograph hanging on the wall comes to his aid. There is Alberto, dressed in a suit, smiling, very different from the man standing with his friend before the half-opened door.

The man dusts off his memories. "Ah, yes, Doctor Granados, now I remember!" The doctor extends his hand and smiles in a friendly but still somewhat disoriented manner. "Come inside then, you must be thirsty; have a seat."

They are given something to drink and they chat. The new arrivals explain they want to visit Machu Picchu, and the doctor arranges for their transportation. The trip will be made on a special train, a cog railway that can climb steep grades.

Ernesto feels asthma twisting up his chest; Alberto gives him an injection and they continue. Later Alberto's aching joints begin to bother him. They certainly miss the motorcycle. En route to Machu Picchu, they meet the manager of a tourist hotel under construction.

The man's intellectual background makes him quite interesting. He tells them he lives where he does because of his leftist ideas, banished, in a way, by Manuel Odría, president of the republic at the time.

Seeing that the manager has in his hands a book about the founding fathers of Latin America, Ernesto—who, according to Granados, was always a Bolivarian—begins a discussion. Far from extolling Bolívar, he extols San Martín. The conversation goes well; their new acquaintance takes a liking to them and asks them to stay for a while. But how can they stay with the Huayna Picchu (Young Peak) and the Machu Picchu (Old Peak) ahead of them?

On the road, they think about what the manager told them about the use of coca in the time of the Incas. It was grown to be given exclusively to couriers on their long journeys. Upon their arrival, the Spaniards were not ignorant of this phenomenon. Coca alleviates hunger, fatigue and thirst. The Spaniards would use it with other ends in mind.

Hundreds of years later, as if they were immune to the cold and hunger, the descendants of the colorful Incas of yore pass by, unaware of the presence of these two Argentines who have come to Machu Picchu. Like the habitual poncho, they carry with them the weight of centuries of exploitation.

Coca leaves and helplessness form part of their daily diet, like that of almost all the dispossessed of the altiplano; this is one of many negative legacies of the colonizer. They become stupified at a low cost, needing only a bit of bicarbonate to make the coca more alkaline so they don't burn their mouths, as if they were unaware or wished to forget that they suffer deeper wounds. This is the way Ernesto and Granados, on their way to Machu Picchu, see the Indians as they pass by.

The ruins are impressive. They stubbornly struggle to survive, pitting their magnificence against time. Ernesto and Granados find them just as Hiram Bingham found them on July 24, 1911. They want to record their presence there and decide to use their camera. One of the photographs they take is of Ernesto standing by one of the doors leading to the Intihuatana—the Incan Sun Temple.

Fatigued, they reach the sacrificial stone. Alberto lies down on the famous stone and talks with his friend, who lights a fire to make maté.

Alberto extemporizes about his vision of forming a workers' center in the Andes, and after winning control of the government, making a revolution for these poor people on the fringe of civilization. It would be good, he asserts, to launch an agrarian reform and an educational reform. Ernesto listens to him and on his lips that ironic smile so typical of him takes form. Deliberately, and with a touch of sympathy, he addresses his friend.

"But Mial, a revolution with no shots fired? Man, have you gone crazy?"

The beauty and simplicity of the location will remain clearly etched in their minds, to such an extent that Ernesto will draw on his memories of it years later in his work as a journalist. Each nook, each stone, set in place with limitless mastery, fills them with awe.

They look for a way to return to Cuzco; from there they intend to go to Huánuco, where there is a leprosarium.

On the Way Back to Lima

They're on their way back to the city. Their stay in Huánuco lasted four days. In the leprosarium they asked for the doctor in charge, but found out he was no longer there, that he had returned to Lima. A patient with quite a bit of training had taken his place. They were told that in the short time he was there, Doctor Pesce carried out some worthy research. He discovered an outbreak of leprosy and did work related to the physiology of the Indian. He also found exanthematous typhus there; it's not a common typhoid, but rather, a type of typhus that is spread by fleas in one's clothes.

Doctor Pesce's work made the institution an important focus of scientific interest. The news wasn't well received by President Odría, who had sent the physician to that secluded spot, removing him from his professorship in tropical medicine at the university. A certain word appeared in the doctor's dossier: communist.

When Ernesto and Granados learned about the scientist's ideas about society they became even more interested in meeting him. At the leprosarium, the two travelers once more came into contact with the deplorable conditions in which indigenous people lived. They had a number of other experiences that were no less important to them, including a meeting with the medical personnel. They were asked several times to stay on.

Going It Alone

Once more the night has come and they haven't reached their destination. With nowhere to sleep, the only place they can try is the local jail. Their experience there will surpass the limits of their patience.

At the precinct, the prisoners' hands move agilely. Colors combine. Ponchos are the end product of the prisoners' labor. It doesn't take Ernesto and Granados long to find out that the profits from the sale of these items end up in the hands of the chief or deputy chief of police.

The women who visit the prisoners wait their turn with the patience that seems to identify their race. Each is wearing four or five petticoats, making their dresses look very bulky. Unscrupulous guards expose the women's breasts to everyone present. The women keep silent, while the guards, filled with lust, begin to paw over their bodies and even rub their genitals on the pretext of searching them.

Granados and Ernesto are witnesses. There are sparks of anger in their eyes at such humiliation. A storm is in the making, and it will burst out when an Indian woman walking along the corridor reaches the guard.

The visitors can't believe their eyes. The girl's scream—she's actually more child than woman—jolts them. The man next to her has raised her dress and his fingers, like rabid worms, search for her genital organs. The scream is an accusation. Granados cries out, "Look at that animal! You have to be totally insensible to put up with that shithead, that imbecile!"

The guard interrupts his dirty work. "What's with you? Do you want to be sent to a cell like the rest?" he asks, gesturing with his head toward the Indians.

"You and who else are going to put me in a cell?" Granados defiantly inquires.

His authority challenged, the man blurts out, "Do you want to see how I shoot you? Do you want to see it right here and now?"

"Yes, I want to see it," Alberto answers, and he feels the cold metal of the revolver he is carrying, hidden on his body. He has the sensation of feeling the whole shape of the weapon on his skin, and his voice has gone up a pitch. "Yes, I want to see it! I want to see it!"

The Indians immerse themselves more deeply in the heavy silence; this seems to heighten the anger of the guard, who approaches the young men. The two appear to be waiting for him, and he stops at a prudent distance and says, "Get the hell out of here."

71

They leave the station. When they are alone, Ernesto turns to his friend. "What an idiot you are, Runt. I mean, do you really believe you, alone, can solve something that all these people haven't been able to solve yet?"

They head toward Oxapampa. The area is picturesque, almost like a tropical jungle bordering on mountains. On the way, Granados ponders the words of his friend: "... you alone, Runt."

Afterward they go to Lima to personally meet Doctor Pesce.

Always Telling the Truth

The meeting with Doctor Pesce couldn't have been better. The recent arrivals tell him about the vicissitudes of their journey, and the scientist sympathizes with them. He takes them to the leprosarium where he works and gives them a place to stay there. They establish a working relationship with the rest of the personnel there devoid of formalities. They work and they learn. Pesce tells them of his experiences and they show themselves to be enthusiastic and receptive.

In the evenings, they visit the city and have a good time. Ernesto meets a social worker, and they become friends. One day, soon before they depart, she gives him a striped sweater and a camping stove. Since the food in the leprosarium isn't the greatest. Doctor Pesce invites them to dine at his house on a number of occasions. There they meet his wife and son. In a conversation over supper, Pesce tells them proudly that he has written a book entitled *Latitudes of Silence*. He brings up the subject of his book over and over again.

Before leaving, they tell Pesce about the route they plan to follow: They'll try to cross the Amazon to San Pablo and work in the leprosarium there for fifteen or twenty days. The physician puts them in touch with an official who is in charge of a fleet of trucks covering the Lima-Pucallpa route. With that business solved, the only thing left for them to do there is to bid farewell and attend a dinner that Pesce has prepared for them in his house.

The meal is delicious, the atmosphere pleasant. Hungry, they eat ravenously, chatting all the while.

"Hey, you haven't said anything about my book."

Alberto wants to encourage him: "Your book, Doctor, is very interesting. It describes the Indian and his fatalistic spirit very well. There are good anecdotes in it about Indian life. Yes, your book really is very interesting."

The response pleases him, but he wants to round it out with Ernesto's opinion. "And what do you think of my book?"

Ernesto is eating his soup. He hears the question and pauses, holding his spoon halfway between the bowl and his mouth. He looks into Pesce's eyes and says nothing. The habitual noises of the house cease. The silence grows. Alberto tries to break the spell: "Ah, the part in which you describe the flooding of the river, that part is full of life!"

Pesce appears enthusiastic. The plates are no longer being passed from hand to hand; the supper is reaching its end. Coffee has been poured, steam is rising from the cups, and Pesce, scientist to the end, persists: "Ernesto, will you finally tell me what you think of my book?"

The answer is silence, a heavy, sticky silence, slow and solemn. Alberto, not daring to speak again, raises his coffee cup to his lips. Ernesto continues to look at Pesce. Someone begins to clear the dishes from the table and take them to the kitchen. The conversation turns to a more mundane subject.

When the visit reaches its end, everyone moves toward the door. They are wished a successful journey. Everything seems fine, but the scientist takes the plunge: "Ernesto, how can you leave without giving me your opinion about the book? I'm listening."

Ernesto stops and swallows, almost imperceptibly; even so, his voice sounds deliberate and cautious.

"Listen, Doctor. It seems impossible that a man so intelligent as yourself, with your ability and courage, could have written so mediocre a book. The book is bad because it's negative, because it's not Marxist, because it gives a description of the Indians' fatalism that isn't truthful because it is from our point of view and not theirs."

Ernesto speaks to him without constraint and Pesce listens to him in silence, like a big child who knows he has done something wrong and all of a sudden is confronted face to face with it. The ideas fall like a heavy, steady rain from which there is no protection. "You are quite right, Ernesto," the doctor admits.

They shake hands and depart. The two friends walk toward the hospital. To get there they have to walk some sixty blocks; although it's a nice night for a walk, neither of them feels comfortable. Ernesto has his hands in his pockets, and Alberto moves his with contained rage as he walks, as if he would like to punch the wind, freeing himself from the discomfort that possesses him. They reach a bridge and both of them stop. They watch the water running; all that can be heard is the voice of the current.

Alberto suddenly bursts out: "Look Pelao, you're a son of a bitch! The poor old guy has given us food, he's given us money, he's given us a place to stay, he's arranged for our transportation, the only thing that concerned him was his book, and look what you tell him!"

Ernesto looks at his friend and his features change; he knits his brow and speaks in an almost inaudible voice, more for himself than for his friend. "But Runt, didn't you see that I didn't want to talk?" he says, almost as if he were reproaching himself for that trait of his of being incisive, always speaking the truth.

A Valley, an Accident, Pisco and a Discussion

The truck caravan is heading toward the north. Alberto asks his friend how he's feeling, and Ernesto answers that he's better. A few hours before they left Lima he was struck by a punishing asthma attack.

Two Professionals Waste Their Time

The scenery is powerful, like the legs of the llamas that travel these roads. Occasionally they hear the voice of one of the drivers singing a tango. Who might he be, that person bringing back memories of Argentina?

A virgin forest surrounds them; they still know little about it. But the marvelling of the travelers reaches new heights when they see the Tingo Maria valley. It is a lovely gift from nature, a mountain with forms like a sleeping woman, as if it were waiting for the caress of the traveler's eyes.

Everything feels new to them, even the inhabitants of the area. The people are more given to conversation and joking; one can see in them the mix of Indian and Black.

On one of the caravan's compulsory stops, they have the opportunity to meet the man who was singing the tango, the title of which is "Siglo XX."

"What's your name?" Alberto inquires. The man looks at him congenially and answers that it is "Cambalache" (or "second-hand shop").

"After the tango?"

"Yes, after the tango, although that's not its real name, but everyone knows it as Cambalache. Want a drink?"

Cambalache pushes a bottle of Peruvian pisco toward him. Alberto takes a slug and licks his lips in pleasure. Before much time has passed, the procedure has been repeated several times. He hands the bottle to Ernesto, but Ernesto declines.

The conversation is pleasant, as is the taste of the pisco, which has left a blush on Alberto's face. Cambalache begins to softly hum a tango and Alberto joins him. With the song and the pisco, voices seem to come alive; one and all join in on the chorus. As the drink flows, the pitch changes; before long they are singing way out of key. The driver's brother is part of the group, and they call him Cambalache too. Both he and Alberto have had too much to drink; Ernesto admonishes his friend.

"Hey man, what does it matter if I'm drunk or I'm not if we're having a good time?" says Alberto, and he continues singing. His friend watches him, but the alcohol has muddled Alberto's senses to the point that he is unaware of Ernesto's gaze, which under other circumstances he would have understood in an instant. He feels as agile and energetic as ever; he walks but doesn't feel his legs wobbling.

"Come on, Runt, enough for today," says Ernesto.

His friend, who has his back toward him, slowly turns his head to face him. He squints, as if he were having difficulty recognizing Ernesto. Finally he manages to gather his thoughts: "Look Pelao, you seem like an old man; if you're bored like an old man then go to sleep, but let me have a good time." And he continues with a string of not-too-flattering words.

"You're a big boy and you know what you're doing; I'm going," says Ernesto, and making a half turn, he moves toward his cot. It's late at night when Alberto finally turns in to sleep it off.

Everyone is on their feet early in the morning; one could hear the sound of the motors. As they eat breakfast, one of the Cambalaches asks Alberto in a facetious tone if he wants to sing a tango. They exchange ideas. Alberto is lucid, but he's a little embarrassed by the incident. With one of the brothers named after the tango, Ernesto discusses the reasons men get drunk. Someone suggests that some people do it out of a lack of interest in life, and others because they are unable to set goals for their future.

Ernesto, jumping headlong into the debate, expresses his point of view that the drinking habit of many uneducated men is passed on from the possessing class, which urges such vices on them in order to keep them alienated.

Alberto listens to him talk and realizes, silently, that his friend is extraordinarily wise for his age. He looks at him affectionately, and his words make him feel even greater pain; he is proud of his friend, but regrets having learned this lesson at such a high price. Ernesto understands and gives him a hand, putting an arm around his shoulder and prodding him on: "Come on, Runt, the trucks are about to go and they'll leave us behind. Hurry up."

The bumpy ride jolts their cramped muscles. After seemingly endless hours, they finally reach Pucallpa. Formerly, rubber and chicle from jungle plantations passed through here, but now only a few buildings of wood and masonry give a sense of the splendor of the town's past.

There is a dance that night, and the friends decide to go. It's a bustling crowd, and the couples seem to multiply on the dance floor. Ernesto approaches his friend and tells him in a low voice, "Runt, listen well. I'm going to dance, but you know..." Alberto doesn't need any kind of explanation to know that his friend is incapable of distinguishing a military march from a milonga. "When they play a tango," Ernesto requests, "kick me, then I'll know what it is. Agreed?"

More or less every other piece played by the improvised band is a tango, but for some reason they suddenly play a Brazilian shoro entitled "Delicado." Granados remembers the song was very popular at the time his friend began to court Chichina, and wishing to remind him of that time, taps him with his foot.

Ernesto takes a young woman out to dance. The tempo of the shoro is quick, but he doesn't hear it. He dances to the beat of a tango, marking off his steps with mathematical precision.

Alberto watches him and can't hold back his laughter. Ernesto notices his friend's behavior, and behind the back of his dancing partner, signals with his hand, as if to ask why he is laughing.

When the song ends, Granados explains to his friend that he was laughing so hard he was unable to say anything. Ernesto doesn't worry about it: he himself laughs at his lack of talent as a dancer.

Later the toasts begin. The pisco goes down smoothly but takes its effect. Alberto has too much to drink and feels the room begin to spin around him, together with the couples—over sixty of them—still dancing. It's already late when they head off to bed.

With the Yagua Indians

Tired, they flop down on the bed, but the mosquitoes don't let them rest. It's not yet dawn, and they're already being told it's time to set out on their journey. Accompanying them are the director of the leprosarium and one of the patients, an Indian by descent.

They board a motorboat at the San Pablo docks and take off in the direction of Iquitos. They travel for about an hour, before leaving the Amazon and heading down a small stream in a rowboat. After navigating for an hour, they disembark and enter the heart of the jungle. Swarms of insects force them to roll down the sleeves of their shirts.

The promiscuousness of the Yagua, when the meet them, surprises them. Any cacique can keep six or seven women, as many as he can support. Their huts, made from palm leaves, leave much to be desired. Ernesto and Alberto can stand being in them only for a short time because of the odor; in order to keep the mosquitoes away, the Indians smear themselves with certain types of fat, mainly alligator fat, and the visitors are not accustomed to the penetrating odor.

As a sign of welcome, the Indians invite the two friends to join them on a monkey hunt. Years later, while in Guatemala, Ernesto would write about this experience in a Sunday supplement to a local newspaper.

At sunset, the hunters are already suitably stationed, hidden by the vegetation of the jungle. Two of the men will shoot at the prey, aided by several women who are given the task of finding the monkey when he's been shot down. They need a great deal of agility to do this, since the monkey can easily be lost in the vegetation.

The weapons are elementary, but, in the hands of the Yagua, accurate: blow guns, about 1.8 meters in length, with which they shoot 40-centimeter-long darts covered with a substance very similar to the nux vomica seed, which paralyzes the nervous system.

Granados and Ernesto experience an adventure on their own continent as fascinating as any contained in the books of Salgari. They wait, impatiently, together with the Inidans, wondering if the hunters haven't picked the wrong spot. One of the Indians tells them to look at the foliage. They learn that it's not so difficult to find the place where the monkeys pass. By eating the most tender leaves and shoots of the treetops, the monkeys open a narrow path of light in the impenetrable jungle, exposing their trail.

In the distance the hunters hear a cackling din, which, as it grows louder, sounds more like barking. A short time later the monkeys begin to pass by. The procession seems as though it will never end. The hunters are relaxed. Seeing the number of monkeys that have come and gone, Granados wonders if they are going to let them all go. But the Indians clearly didn't learn how to hunt yesterday; they know what they're doing.

Three or four more monkeys pass by and the Indians finally raise the blow guns to their mouths. Behind, far behind, come two of the animals. Each hunter chooses his target. The sound of the shooting is almost imperceptible; two bodies fall in the undergrowth and the women go into action. The pack continues on its path and doesn't notice its losses. The following day they would come back by the same route.

When the hunters return to the settlement, the two visitors are invited to share eating the day's catch. Ernesto remains pensive; Alberto accepts for the two of them. The smell of food is in the air and the travelers are getting hungry. Amid banter, they go to the table and are taken aback at the way the food is served. Surrounded by cooked yucca and seasoned with lots of hot chili peppers, the two monkeys look like babies, only a couple of months old. They see the director of the leprosarium trying to conceal his laughter. The hospitality of the Indians helps them pull themselves together and pluck up their courage to eat. They are also served *masao*, a drink the Indians make by fermenting yucca with saliva.

That night they learn something new about the Yagua. Although they are friendly, the men don't like anyone sleeping near their women. The two friends find they have to sleep in the boat. The next day, for breakfast, they eat monkey meat once again.

Back in the leprosarium watching the inhabitants cross the Amazon in rafts, it occurs to them that perhaps they could do the same. The leprosarium patients take a fairly large, unusable raft and rebuild it for them, baptizing it the *Mambo-Tango*.

The wife of the director of the leprosarium, learns of their plans. "Have you gone crazy? How can two scientists travel down a river in a raft?"

The other employees react the same way, but nobody can convince the two friends to change their minds. They listen to instructions on how to propel the raft with a pole and are told to always stay close to the right bank of the river where the military posts are, so the military knows they are not smugglers attempting to elude them.

The past twelve days have touched both the hosts and visitors deeply. When Ernesto tells one of the patients that they are thinking of leaving the following day, the man looks at him sadly, and after consulting with his fellow patients, he comes to Ernesto and says, "Tonight you must meet us at the director's dock. We'll see you there."

A light rain is falling that evening in San Pablo, and there is fog. Granados and Ernesto can see the patients arriving in their boats. They sing a Peruvian song they had dedicated to Ernesto on the night of his birthday a few days earlier. Then the employees' band plays another song, producing an interesting melodic counterpoint between the two musical groups.

One of the patients speaks words of thanks and praise for the two doctors who have come and stayed in such a remote location. He says they will never forget the two men's warm, unrestrained behavior toward them, and the fact that they didn't use gloves or masks when treating them.

The two friends look at each other hesitantly, not certain what they should say or which of the two should speak to the gathering. Granados takes the floor; he's almost become an expert at farewells, but even he is moved by the patients' expressions of affection. He feels tongue-tied and his voice falters, but he manages to piece together his ideas, and ends up speaking for a long time.

Later, on board their vessels, the patients ride off into the whitish fog, singing. The words to the song say something about a farewell forever. The boats disappear beyond the horizon, but the song remains in the air, hovering in the rain. Up to that moment the two friends had believed such visions occur only in dreams.

Heading toward the dormitory, Ernesto and Alberto can't refrain from talking about how their ties of friendship with the patients arose. They remember the reaction of a man carrying a bunch of bananas when Pelao said to him, "If I may," and took one, peeled it and began to eat it.

"But Doctor, what about your gloves? What about your mask?" the patient burst out.

"Don't worry friend, that's nonsense, I don't need them," he answered, and continued as if nothing had happened.

Sports were another way the barriers of mistrust were tossed aside.

That night they talked at length. Pelao spoke about how sensitive the patients were—hypersensitive, in fact—to any friendly gesture or act from a healthy individual, how for them a smile could be a precious gift. He kept on talking, delivering the speech he hadn't given at the farewell—but which had been expressed through his behavior.

Early in the morning they left aboard the *Mambo-Tango*. They took photos; in the face of the director of the leprosarium they sensed a desire to join them.

On the Amazon

The *Mambo-Tango*, propelled by pole, proceeds to their next destination, Letizia, a port located on the border of Peru, Brazil and Colombia. From there they plan to go to Bogotá.

The director of the leprosarium has given them provisions for five or six days, even though the travelers believe they'll arrive at their destination in only two or three. With the sun climbing high in the sky, the crew of two seeks refuge under the palm-leaf roof that was built to protect them from inclement weather. They're hungry, and Ernesto goes to what could be considered the stern of the craft, where the raft-builders had placed some clay, on top of which a fire can be lit.

It's not easy to navigate on the Amazon, especially when the navigators aren't experts; the instructions they were given must be followed to the letter. The force of the current pushes them toward the other bank. They must react quickly. They also have to fight off clusters of trunks and underbrush that float with the current, pushing them away with poles before they become entangled with the raft. They divide their forces: One takes charge of the helm and the other fights the underbrush.

They create a system for keeping watch at night, taking turns every three hours. The *Mambo-Tango* challenges the Amazon and slowly advances. The light of their lantern not only warns them of any danger, but it also allows the military control posts to see them.

During the day they try to take maximum advantage of the sunlight. They devour books and discuss them. The scenery and its beauty hold their attention. Every once in a while they try their luck at fishing. They have a large hook and line, and one day, just to pass the time and see what happens, they toss the hook overboard, using the neck of a chicken as bait. Soon the line draws abruptly taut. At first they think it might have gotten caught on a submerged tree trunk, but their doubts evaporate when they see the line move from side to side. The struggle begins. The fish leaps into the air; it's a huge *saltón*, a fish that can weigh as much as fifty or sixty pounds, and it doesn't want to leave the Amazon. Granados and Ernesto haul in the line. The fish drags the *Mambo-Tango* toward the opposite bank. Time passes and the safety of the rustic vessel is endangered. Finally they have to take a knife and cut the line.

Hours and days pass as they float down the river. Diaries are brought up to date. One morning they're eating a huge and juicy pineapple. Having cut it in two, they raise it to their mouths and the sweet juice rolls off their beards and falls on their chests.

"Listen, Fuser: There's no doubt that travel greatly improves one's culture. Just look at our manners!" The two laugh. The freedom from formality and protocol suits them well. The raft heads downstream in the strong current. Sometimes they think they are approaching an island, but when they draw close enough they can see that what they thought was an island is no more than an enormous mass of underbrush.

Having decided to disembark in Letizia as fashionably as possible, they put on the new clothes that Doctor Pesce had given them. Ernesto wears the striped sweater that was a gift from his friend in Lima; he doesn't change his pants.

But not everything happens as planned. Without realizing it, they pass beyond Letizia, finally docking at the house of a Brazilian man, to whom they explain their situation. They ask him to take them to Letizia, offering the raft in exchange. The man agrees, and they return to the Amazon, this time heading upstream. The Brazilian travels in the bow, Ernesto in the middle and Granados in the stern.

Upon their arrival, the immigration authorities ask them how they made the trip. "On a raft," they tell the officials, who listen in disbelief. At the time Letizia was so remote it could be reached only by seaplane.

Wandering around looking for work, they learn that the town has around 2,000 inhabitants. There are few job options available: fishing, working in the government bureacracy or joining the military. Living conditions are far from ideal; in some areas land is granted to whoever is willing to try to establish himself there. The insects and parasites are awesome foes.

Thanks to the growing popularity of soccer, Ernesto and Granados are hired as managers of Sporting, one of three teams that will compete in the preliminary round of the national military team championship. Ernesto's efforts bear fruit; his team comes out the winner. In the deciding game he plays goalkeeper, a position that's not his strength, forcing him to rely on his rugby-playing experience. During the match he would rush forward, far from the goal; since the players tended to advance the ball too quickly, he could cut them off, throw himself on the ball and avoid further complications.

Sporting's victory wins them the fare for a seaplane ride to Bogotá, a city where unforeseen and unpleasant events await them.

Dagger as Pretext

Almost one month after Ernesto's birthday, they head for Bogotá, the capital city of Colombia. Upon their arrival, they visit the Argentine consul, who treats them kindly. Then they visit a professor who is involved in the fight against leprosy. The scientist finds them a place to stay in a boarding school run by nuns. They leave their bags there and head out again to walk around the city streets.

Not knowing the city, they get lost. Taking the Argentine consulate as a reference point, they try unsuccessfully to find their way. They exchange impressions; Ernesto takes out his letter opener, which is also an Argentine dagger known as a *facón,* and with it he begins to draw the route he thinks they should follow on the rough surface of a wall.

"Who are you?" asks a police officer who has been watching them.

Granados and Ernesto show him their passports. When he sees they are Argentines, one a student and the other a doctor, the policeman stares at them with suspicion.

"All right, your papers are in order," he says, "but give me that weapon." Without hesitating, Ernesto sticks the *facón* under his belt.

"Look, no one takes this from me."

"No? Then you're under arrest!"

They are taken to a station called a *permanente,* often used during the reign of Laureano Gómez to jail citizens. These are so common that there is a *permanente* practically on every corner.

An hour and a half later Granados speaks to one of the policemen at the station.

"Very well, gentlemen, why are we being held here? Why don't you let us go?"

"Shut up!" the policeman orders.

"Why should we shut up?" Ernesto chimes in. The situation becomes tense.

"Give it to him! Hit him with your rifle butt!" says one policeman, while the other makes a move to hit Ernesto.

"Go ahead! I dare you!" the young man challenges.

A corporal who has been listening to the commotion addresses Ernesto politely, asking him for the weapon. Ernesto obeys.

A short time later they are ordered to get into a paddy wagon and are driven around a few blocks in order to intimidate them. Finally set free, they make contact with a group of students and narrate their encounter.

"Ah, you're lucky!" they are told. "The police kill people here for less than that!"

They visit the consul, hoping to enlist his aid in recovering the weapon. The diplomat, however, reacts with alarm: "Have you gone crazy? They'll kill you! You can't do that in this country!"

And he continues, describing the situation in Colombia. Since the appearance of guerrilla groups in the country, he tells them, anyone with leftist ideas is assassinated with impunity.

They say goodbye and, once in the streets, talk the situation over. After weighing the possible consequences of acting on the matter, they decide to return to the police station. Before they do that, however, they pick up two students, who wait for them outside the station.

They ask to speak to the lieutenant, and he receives them. The officer explains to them that the policeman in question claimed they had tried to assault him, which demonstrated a lack of respect and is a very serious matter.

"Listen, the policeman can say what he wants, but we never tried to assault him," says Ernesto.

"That weapon cannot be taken from here! That weapon doesn't leave this station! It doesn't leave!" the policeman screams.

"Look, a bit of advice," warns the officer. "What you should do is leave the country, you've already caused problems in Bogotá and you're not welcome here."

"Okay, we'll go," says Ernesto, "but only after you've returned the *facón*. If you give me my knife, we leave. If you don't give it to me, we stay."

The lieutenant opens a drawer and reluctantly throws the *facón* onto the table. Ernesto calmly picks the weapon up and puts it under his belt.

"That's not the end of this!" warns the policeman.

The young men turn their backs on him and walk out the door. After explaining to the students what happened, one student advises, "Take the first bus leaving for Venezuela. Leave soon!"

"We haven't the money to leave!" Ernesto argues, letting the fact that they really don't want to leave show through.

"How can we go now," Granados protests, "if we just learned of a very good poet named Barba Jacob, and we want to visit a leprosarium in Aguas de Dios?"

"Do you want to know something?" one student says. "My opinion is that you shouldn't even spend the night here."

Disturbed, they decide to visit the Argentine consul again. When the official discovers what had happened, he lets out a cry to holy heaven: "That policeman is going to look for you in order to kill you! That's what he's going to do! Kill you!"

They head toward the boarding school and begin to wonder if they really had done something that serious. Abuse and violence pervade Laureano Gómez's Colombia.

Sunday morning arrives. When they get up, the nuns come to their room and ask them, pointedly, "Are you going to mass?"

"No. We're not going to mass today," Alberto responds.

That evening, when they return to their lodgings, they find their bags at the door with a note telling them they can no longer stay there.

The following day the solidarity of the students is demonstrated; they give the two travelers fare to Venezuela. On July 12, they leave Bogotá. They sleep in a small town called Málaga and go from there to Cúcuta.

Cúcuta is a port of entry for both Colombians and Venezuelans; Ernesto and Alberto take an interest in the range of people living there. Some are on their way to the land of Bolívar; others are smugglers. Some of the people there are returning to a normal life after having been cheated in the diamond mines of the Orinoco.

They set out once again and are taken in by the grandeur of the scenery. On the Pan American Highway they catch a glimpse of the eternal snows of Bolívar Peak; half an hour later they are in a tropical climate. Those making the trip for the first time find themselves enthralled by the abrupt changes, not only in scenery but in the political and social climate. They are happy to see an open library in San Antonio de Táchira. They cross central Venezuela and arrive in Caracas.

Touring the streets, the two try to absorb everything; after having traveled so far, their desire to see things with their own eyes has yet to be quenched. The travelers receive good news in the Venezuelan capital. Alberto finds out that a Doctor Convit, whom he had met in Buenos Aires, has been named National Director of the Struggle against Leprosy, Skin Disease and Syphilis. Ernesto, for his part, discovers that an aunt of his who was also his good friend in adolescence, is in Caracas, working in the educational field. Their situation has taken a turn for the better.

Ernesto's aunt finds them lodgings. She sends them to a rather inexpensive boarding house with a letter of recommendation to the manager. They're wearing the same clothes that in other places have caused them more than one misfortune. The manager reads the letter and immediately picks up the telephone.

"Doctor Calvento? These are the 'gentlemen' you sent along?"

"Yes, those are the 'gentlemen,'" Ernesto's aunt answers. "They are neither bad nor dangerous; you can trust them. They just have ideas about life that are a little different from ours."

A third coincidental meeting leads the two to embark on separate paths. Ernesto meets an airplane pilot—a friend of his uncle—who transports race horses on the Buenos Aires-Caracas-Miami-Buenos Aires route.

Granados tells Ernesto he'll stay and find work in a leprosarium. He reminds him to keep his promise to his mother, Celia, to finish his medical studies.

It is agreed that Ernesto will go to Miami, and from there to Buenos Aires to return to medical school. Afterwards, Ernesto will come back and they will work together.

Ernesto's aunt puts them in contact with the UPI correspondent in Venezuela to help Ernesto get his entrance visa for the United States. The meeting with the journalist takes place in Doctor Calvento's house. The conversation covers a number of topics, finally turning to politics. The UPI correspondent suggests it is a pity that the Argentines defeated the English in 1812; if they hadn't, he says, perhaps the Argentines would be like the North Americans.

"Perhaps," Granados observes ironically, "but then again we may have been like the Indians, full of misery, disease and illiteracy."

Ostensibly refuting his friend's argument, Ernesto, who had been silent up to that time, is actually thinking more about what the UPI reporter had said. "I would rather be an illiterate Indian living in misery," he says, "than an American millionaire."

An argument breaks out and Ernesto spares no words. He knows his visa to enter the United States is in jeopardy, but he can't restrain himself.

A few days later, the two friends separate. Alberto watches the plane disappear in the distance. He feels sad, but he's certain they'll see each again soon, because Fuser doesn't go back on his word.

Alberto finds work in Maiquetía, carrying out research on protein electrophoresis for lepers, an advanced technique at the time. He prepares for Ernesto's return; both men have plans to carry out experiments with animals to see if leprosy involves an allergic reaction. He constantly talks to his new friends in Maiquetía about Pelao and even finds him a post as an intern.

What he can't foresee is that years will pass before he sees his friend, and by then Pelao will no longer be called Pelao.

Buenos Aires

More than one of Ernesto's friends and family are surprised to see him return by plane, without Granados. He has a difficult task ahead of him, having to pass exams in more than fifteen subjects. A mountain of books faces him during the month of September.

He often goes to 2208 Arenales and settles in on the fifth floor, where his Aunt Beatriz lives. Gone is the Teté that she rocked to sleep in her arms, humming a lullaby. Now Ernesto himself is bothered by hair hanging over his forehead, and he keeps it cut short. The boy who shuns protocol and loves poetry, the young man who can't stand to put on a necktie—he's the one who climbs the stairs to Beatriz's home.

His aunt is happy to have him there. She watches him as he becomes absorbed in his books. On some nights that winter she makes him as many as twenty cups of maté. This is one habit he'll keep for the rest of his life. He finds other belongings unnecessary, but the maté and the metal straw, as well as the vaporizer to relieve his asthma, fulfill essential needs.

Slowly but surely he passes his exams, and his thesis about allergies takes form. In April 1953, he receives the certificate accrediting him as a doctor of medicine.

Some think Ernesto will now abandon his footloose ways and settle down in Buenos Aires. They would like to see him develop a practice with a stable clientele. Though certainly quite able to do so, he has chosen another path; he'll return to Venezuela to meet Alberto.

There is a farewell party. Here, as at the outset of the first journey, the skeptics crack their jokes, and he laughs. On the eve of his departure, he walks down Avenida San Martín with José Aguilar. This will be their last long conversation before Ernesto leaves Buenos Aires. He has a 6,000-kilometer train ride to La Paz, Bolivia, ahead of him. Almost fourteen years later he'll visit the Bolivian capital once again.

4

WE WILL GO WITH YOU

To your health, Guevara!
Or better still, from the American depths:
Wait for us. We will go with you. We want
to die in order to live as you have died,
to live as you live,
Che Comandante,
friend.

—Nicolás Guillén

Dear folks,
I'm fine
I spent only two and have
five left.
I'm still working
on the same thing. The
news is sporadic
and will continue
being so but have faith
that God is Argentine.
A hug for
all

Tete

A Change of Profession

Don Ernesto

When he finished his studies in April 1953, he told us of his decision to travel around America again. Having made this decision, he left Buenos Aires for Bolivia, Peru, Panama, Costa Rica and Guatemala. During his stay in this last country, the "revolution" of Castillo Armas took place, and he played an active role defending the government of Jacobo Arbenz.

Che

No. I never held a position in that government. But when the U.S. invasion took place, I tried to organize a group of young men like me to confront the adventurers of the United Fruit Company.

Darío López (Cuban exile)

The first time I saw Che was in Guatemala. He wore worn-out shoes and almost always wore the same shirt, part of it hanging out, part tucked in. That day I believe he was on his way to the hospital where he worked. It was when he had only one change of clothes and he was in the habit of asking a *compañero,* "Do you have a shirt or a pair of pants you can lend me?" Sometimes the pants were too big for him, but he put them on anyway and went out into the street. Matters of appearance were of secondary importance to him.

Don Ernesto

After finding asylum in the Argentine embassy in Guatemala, he moved to Mexcio and got back into the rhythm of studying, once again devoting himself to the study of allergies.

Fidel Castro

It was a day in the month of July or August 1955 when I met Che. And one night—as he himself has said in his diaries—he decided to become a member of our expedition.

Che

I met him on one of those cold Mexican nights, and I remember that our first discussion dealt with international politics. But I would like to clarify how and why I met Fidel in Mexico. It was during the ebb of democratic governments in 1954, when the last revolutionary American democracy in this region that remained on its feet—that of Jacobo Arbenz Guzmán—succumbed to the premeditated, cold aggression carried out by the United States behind the smoke screen of its continental propaganda. Its visible mastermind was the Secretary of State, [John] Foster Dulles, who, by strange coincidence, was also a lawyer and stockholder of the United Fruit Company, the main existing imperialist enterprise in Guatemala.

One left there in defeat, united with all Guatemalans in their pain, hoping, searching for a way to remake a future for that anguished country. And Fidel came to Mexico looking for neutral ground where he could train his men for the big push in Cuba.

Don Ernesto

When he was imprisoned we found out about his temporarily abandoning his scientific studies and his adherence to the revolutionary venture against the dictator [Fulgencio] Batista.

Mexico City, June 25 (AP)

The Federal Security Police said today that the detention of Cuban exiles here began last Friday. Sources close to the security force, however, claim that the arrests were made earlier.

The security agents announced that the arrested Cubans had confessed that they were planning to assassinate General Batista in an operation in which one of the plotters would most likely have had to sacrifice his life.

Five Cubans were originally detained, according to police. They are: Fidel Castro, Ciro Redondo, Universo Sánchez, Ramiro Valdés and Reinaldo Benítez.

Another 15 Cubans were subsequently arrested on a ranch 35 kilometers outside of Mexico City belonging to Erasmo Rivera, also a Cuban, who managed to escape, the security police reported.

The Cubans practiced shooting and received military instruction on almost a daily basis on the ranch, police officials revealed. Those arrested, according to a list released by the security police, include Tomás Selecto Pinto, Horacio Rodríguez Hernández, Santiago Hirzel, Eduardo Roig, Ernesto Guevara Serna and Almeida Bosque.

Che

I remember explaining my case to him explicitly: a foreigner, illegally in Mexico, facing a whole series of charges. I told him that under no circumstances should the revolution stop because of me, that they could leave me; that I understood the situation, would try to go and fight from wherever they send me, and the only effort they should make is to have me deported to a nearby country and not to Argentina. I also remember Fidel's categorical response: "I won't abandon you."

Fidel Castro

He was one of those persons everyone felt fond of immediately because of his simplicity, his strength of character, his naturalness, his camaraderie, his personality, his originality, even when they were still unaware of the other singular virtues that were chracteristic of him.

Darío López

In Mexico he had only one brown suit. Of course he had other clothes to change to, but only one suit to dress up in and it was so worn he decided to buy another... of the same color!

Che

Vieja, I'm writing to tell you that you are already a grandmother. I have a daughter and her name is Hilda, like my wife.

We Will Go With You

Fidel Castro

So one day, at the end of November 1956, he set out with us on our journey to Cuba. I remember the voyage was very difficult for him since, given the circumstances under which we had to organize our departure, we couldn't even get the medicines he needed. During the whole crossing he suffered from a strong asthma attack, with no relief.

Luis Crespo (*Granma* expedition member)

He came with us as a doctor, but he didn't call himself a doctor; he called himself *"matasanos"* [sawbones; literally, healthy-person killer]. Before too long we ourselves would say, "Where's the *matasanos,* I've got a blister on my foot, *matasanos.*"

It was after we landed when I helped Che for the first time. It happens that I'm the child of an asthmatic; each time I see an asthmatic I remember my family and my father who was asthmatic. So when I ask, they tell me he's over there, in a swamp. People had fallen behind, it turns out, because they couldn't get through that swamp. I go over to where he was and say, "Give me that, let me help you," and he answers, "No way are you going to help me!" But I insist: "You must be tired from the swamp." From the time we were in Mexico we got used to speaking to each other this way, so he says, "Your mother's going to help me! I came to fight, I didn't come for anyone to help me!" He makes it, asthma and all. finally I take off his knapsack and say to him, "Relax, we'll be there in no time."

Don Ernesto

It was then that I began to visualize Ernesto as a warrior. I couldn't get used to the idea. I was always an antimilitarist. That caste of military men at the service of imperialism, who would use their profession to oppress the people, always disgusted me.

When the subject of the military came up I was in the habit of reciting that definitive verse of Rubén Darío—"Free is the brow that refuses the helmet"—and I couldn't really comprehend how a child of mine could choose the "helmet" as the destiny of his life.

Perhaps in my mind I made an error of judgment: An army of barbarians, of mercenaries, like the bulk of Latin American armies, is one thing, and a people who take up arms to defend their liberty is another.

The idea of Ernesto the scientist stayed in my mind, and now, suddenly, it was Ernesto the warrior. Nevertheless, considering the course of his life—in which he had had the opportunity to see first-hand the brutality of human misery—the fact that an outburst of rebelliousness would appear in him, leading him to fight for the liberation of a country, was quite natural.

Little by little the concept of the guerrilla as a person who fights for ideals became clearer to me, and as I gained more clarity on this question, the specter of the professional military "helmet" serving foreign interests receded into the background.

Che

Let us set out,
fiery prophet of the dawn,
on hidden, unlit paths
to liberate the green caiman that you so love.
Let us set out
to rout dishonor with a countenance
replete with insurrectionary stars of Marti,
swearing to gain victory or find death.
When the first shot rings out and the entire jungle awakens
in virgin surprise,
serene combatants there at your side,
you shall have us.
When your voice scatters to the four winds
agrarian reform
justice, bread, liberty,
serene combatants there at your side,
you shall have us.
And when the surgical operation against the tyrant
comes to the end of its course,
there, at your side, awaiting the final battle,

you shall have us.
The day the beast licks his wounded flank
struck by the arrow of nationalization,
there, at your side, with a proud heart,
you shall have us.
Don't you believe that the vermin decorated with medals and
armed with gifts
can diminish our integrity;
we ask for a gun, bullets and a rugged mountain.
Nothing more.
And if on our path cold metal intervenes,
we ask for a shroud of Cuban tears
to cover guerrilla bones
in the passage of America's history.
Nothing more.

Fidel Castro

I believe that in the period in which I met Che, his revolutionary development, ideologically speaking, was more advanced than mine. From a theoretical point of view, he was more educated, he was a more advanced revolutionary than I. But in those days we didn't talk about those matters. What we discussed was the struggle against Batista, the plan to land in Cuba and launch our guerrilla force. And in that situation it was Che's militant temperament, as a man of action, that drove him to join me in the struggle.

Che

It was perhaps the first time that I had to deal with the dilemma of my commitment to medicine and my duty as a revolutionary soldier as a practical question. I had in front of me a knapsack filled with medicines and a box of bullets. Together they were too heavy for me to carry; leaving the knapsack, I took the box of bullets and crossed the clearing that stood between me and the cane fields.

A Battle

Che

On May 25th, we got word that an expedition had landed near Mayarí.

Fidel Castro

Remembering the experience we had landing and the difficult times we had gone through, we wanted to support that group with some sort of military action.

Che

We had an interesting discussion there in which Fidel and the person who writes these lines were the main protagonists. My opinion was that the opportunity to seize a truck shouldn't be lost and that, specifically, we should try to capture one on the roads. But Fidel already had the action of Uvero in mind. He thought capturing the post at Uvero would be much more interesting and a much more resounding success.

Fidel Castro

Che was still the doctor. He had no troops under his command.

Che

Now, several years after that discussion in which Fidel made the decision, but didn't convince me, I must admit that his judgment was sound.

Fidel Castro

Accordingly, we headed for the coast, where an enemy infantry company, protected by armored enclosures and trenches, was stationed.

Alejandro Oñāte Cañete (rebel soldier)

On May 28th, they placed me with the group under Che's command, and we left. Joel Iglesias was with us; together—Joel and I—we helped Che with his machine gun.

Che

I will always remember when they gave me that machine gun. It was of very poor quality and old, but at the time it was a real prize. Four men were assigned to the weapon as assistants; one of them was a 15-year-old child who almost always had to carry the enormous weight of the magazines. His name was Joel Iglesias.

Joel Iglesias

"Can you handle that sack?" Che asked me, pointing to one of the jute sacks filled with machine-gun magazines that had recently arrived in the Sierra.

"Yes, I can handle it," I answered, in order to back up what I had been saying, to convince them to accept me in the Rebel Army. I would tell them that although I was young, I was strong, that I was accustomed to working in the countryside. So that was how I began to work as Che's assistant, together with Alejandro Oñate Cañete ("Cantinflas").

Fidel Castro

At daybreak, we planned the attack rather quickly, with the information we had at our disposal. By that time Che was already with us on the General Staff, he already had some responsibilities.

Che

The General Staff met with all the officers, and Fidel announced that within the next forty-eight hours we would engage in combat. The Uvero military post was located at the edge of the ocean, so to surround it we only needed to attack from three sides.

Fidel Castro

When, at daybreakk, we were about to initiate the battle, we were faced with a complicated situation because the information we had wasn't accurate; the positions weren't exactly where we thought they were, and the set-up was complicated. Nevertheless, we had to carry it out. The various small units, platoons and squads, were waiting around the perimeter of the post, at a distance of a kilometer and half or more. We couldn't pull back. We simply had to attack.

Che

Fidel opened fire with his telescopic sight, and we could make out the outlines of the garrison by the answering fire that began a few seconds later.

Fidel

We had to ask a platoon led by compañero Almeida to advance rapidly toward the post, coming as close as possible to specified positions. It was a very risky move that resulted in a number of casualties.

Che

Everyone moved forward. Almeida moved toward the group that was guarding the entrance to the garrison; on my left we could see Camilo's* cap with a piece of cloth hanging down over the back of his neck, like the hats of the Foreign Legion, but with the initials of our movement. We advanced in the midst of a general firefight, with all the precautions that this type of combat requires.

*Camilo Cienfuegos

Fidel

We also had to make a move toward the west. And as we analyzed what to do and the need to make that move, Che immediately offered to do it. It was the third time when we needed a volunteer that Che made himself available right away. When there is a difficult situation, he takes immediate action.

Joel Iglesias

I knew nothing about war, not even in the movies. The soldiers were hidden behind parapets in a wooden garrison, without much protection; they had a number of machine gun nests and firepower in advantageous, high positions. Next to the post there was some lumber from Babún's sawmill; the soldiers shielded themselves there. Our section, on the other hand, had low, sparse vegetation, so we had to crawl forward so as not to be seen.

Che

We met tough resistance and had reached the flat, open area where we had to move forward with extreme caution, since the enemy fire was continuous and on target. From my position, barely fifty or sixty meters from the enemy's front line, I saw two soldiers leaving the forward trench at full speed and I shot at both of them, but they took refuge in the sugar mill workers' houses, which were off limits for us.

Joel Iglesias

Around two hours of constant fire placed us in a difficult situation. The number of wounded was rising, and Almeida was one of those wounded. The casualties created a sense of shock, which was not very favorable as far as the spirit of those who were fighting was concerned.

Che

At that moment I heard a howl and several cries in the middle of the battle and I thought an enemy soldier had been wounded.

I crawled forward, calling on him to surrender, but it was the *compañero* Leal, wounded in the head. The only bandage I had on me was a piece of paper, which I placed on the wounds. Joel Iglesias went to his side a little later, while we continued our attack.

Joel Iglesias

Sensing the state of dispiritedness, Che stopped crawling forward and stood up with his machine gun at waist level, continuing swiftly toward the garrison.

Luis Alfonso Zavas

He was one of the first ones who entered and forced the troops quartered there to surrender.

Joel Iglesias

He was one of the first to enter the garrison.

Che

We were regaining our courage and gathering our determination to take the post by assault, since it was the only way to put an end to the resistance, when the garrison surrendered.

With the Wounded

Fidel Castro

It was a difficult battle; practically 30 percent of the forces on both sides were wounded or killed. The battle had been inspired by the desire to help those who had landed to the north; despite our efforts, however, they were all surrounded, captured and killed. As a result of that battle—after three hours of fighting and having occupied the camp—a good number of our people and our adversaries were wounded.

Che

When I went to hand over the wounded to the military doctor, he asked me, in quick succession, how old I was and when I had received my degree. I explained to him it was several years earlier, and he said to me frankly, "Listen buddy, you take charge of all this because I just graduated and I have very little experience." At that point I had to exchange my gun once more for a doctor's "uniform" —meaning, simply, that I washed my hands.

Fidel Castro

Che was the doctor who quickly treated the wounded among our soldiers and the enemy soldiers. This was a practice and norm of our entire struggle.

Che

In total, fifteen of our *compañeros* were put out of commission. The enemy had nineteen wounded, fourteen killed, another fourteen taken prisoner, and six escaped.

Fidel Castro

Afterwards, naturally, enemy forces converged. They began to pursue us in force, because after having treated our wounded adversaries, we left them there so they would be picked up by their own forces when we withdrew. Che, as the doctor, stayed with our wounded, cared for them. They were in a remote spot; it was a difficult situation, with a large force in the region trying to surround our column.

Joel Iglesias

When the bulk of the troops withdrew, we remained there, treating the wounded. Then we gathered medicines, food, everything we could, and we left. We buried our dead in the hills and looked for a place where our wounded could recover.

We were five men taking care of Maceo, Hermes, Kike Escalona, Manals, Pena and Manuel Acuña—the first three of whom were in serious shape and had to be carried by hammock. This, plus the fact that planes were searching for us and we were expecting the army to come in pursuit, made our group's situation quite distressing.

Fidel Castro

The column marched through very steep and rugged terrain. We eluded the siege. But Che remained in the rear guard with the wounded and very few men.

Che

We foresaw heavy enemy pursuit and decided that the troops who were able to walk should put as much distance as possible between themselves and the enemy, while I was made responsible for the wounded. My assistants Joel Iglesias and On[ate, a guide named Sinecio Torres, and Vilo Acun[a stayed with me.

Joel Iglesias

It was a difficult stage, we spent all day walking and only moved two or three kilometers; we hardly ate, the wounded were getting worse, it was raining, and the sanitary conditions were poor. Then we found the house of Emelina and Israel, and they helped us; they cooked us a meal that we never got a chance to eat because the couple was detained by the army and couldn't carry the food to the woods. I should point out that they didn't inform on us; they acted bravely.

Manuel Escudero (*campesino* collaborator)

After the Uvero attack, Che sent for me in Los Altos de la Botella and asked me if I wanted to be his messenger. He had a lot of wounded men with him, but the most seriously wounded was Almeida. I saw that they needed someone to help them and said yes, no problem, that I knew all the back paths. That's how I began working with him. Soon a lot of *campesinos* helped me. I told them to act stupid and tell me about the soldiers' movement in the area of San Pablo de Yao. They did it, and I traveled around the backwoods keeping Che informed.

Che

On the bank of the Peladero River there lived an overseer of a large landowner, by the name of David, who collaborated a lot with us.

David Gómez Pliego

Che was reclining on a cedar of about one hundred inches in circumference that stood on the edge of the Peladero River, and as he was talking to me, he took out a lemon and began to eat it, peel and all. He told me that he was very worried about the wounded, who were the most seriously affected, because for three days the troops hadn't eaten a thing due to the danger that smoke from their fires would give their location away. He asked me to slaughter a cow for them and to get them some food and other things they needed.

Che

David slaughtered a cow for us and we had to go get it; we had to move the meat at night.

David Gómez

Since I had to leave the house very early to arrive here on time, I said to him that I brought something to eat and I want to share it with you. He answered that he would save his share for the wounded. I felt myself turning red from shame and I closed the bag with the food, gave it to him and said, "I won't eat breakfast either, take it to the wounded."

When our talk ended, I realized that I was in the presence of an extraordinary man, and when I said goodbye, I gave him a hug because I already felt like one more member of the guerrillas.

Che

During that period I had a long conversation with David, the overseer, who asked me for a list of all the important things we needed. He said he was going to go to Santiago to pick things up for us there. He was a typical overseer: loyal to the owner, contemptuous of the *campesinos,* racist.

David Gómez

Our second meeting took place three days later. I brought him two large portable alcohol stoves, fuel, sugar, coffee and other things. I also told him about the movement of Batista's troops in the region and the questioning I was subjected to at the Uvero garrison, where there were a great number of troops gathered.

I was the overseer of the largest farm in the region and hadn't had any problems up to that point in time, since the soldiers considered me to be their collaborator. I had to pretend to be one, because the most important thing at that point definitely was to save the wounded, some of whom were seriously wounded, such as Kike Escalona and then-Captain Juan Almeida.

I told Che that I was going to ask the army for safe conduct to travel to Santiago to buy medicines for the cattle, food for the workers and other things that I normally bought for the farm. I suggested he give me a list of things he needed so I could bring them back mixed in with my other purchases. Che agreed and spoke to me openly about his doubts about whether I would talk if the troops got wise to me.

Joel Iglesias

With that help, we moved forward more rapidly, on a fixed course. I could talk a long time about how we did it. Almeida, for example, despite having two bullets in his body, walked, dragging himself from tree to tree. We could help very little because some of us always had to bring up the rear, covering up our tracks, watching to make sure we weren't ambushed, and if

106

we were, being ready to cover for the wounded as they withdrew.

Che

At one point we had to look for a cave to leave some food there, since the plan to bring things from Santiago came through and David brought us quite a serious load that we couldn't possibly carry with us, given the state of our troops, made up of convalescents and raw recruits.

David Gómez

Do you know who transported all that? A Navy boat brought it all the way from Santiago to the El Peladero dock. Coastguard cutter number 12. The sailors themselves loaded and unloaded the merchandise. What happened was that I showed the safe-conduct they gave me in Uvero to Colonel Rubí Baró, chief of the Navy in Oriente. That man agreed to help me as long as I paid him with several thousand boards of precious wood—found in abundance on the farm—that he needed for something he was building on his property. I had two trucks filled with sealed wooden boxes; in them, under the medicines for the cattle, were food, medicines and thousands of bullets of various calibers. The sailors loaded it all, and I carried it the rest of the way to my house by mule.

Che

The army imprisoned him after finding out about our contact with him, and they tortured him barbarously. His first concern when he was released—we believed him to be dead—was to explain that he hadn't talked.

David Gómez

They detained me on the basis of a denunciation. They applied the *"combinada,"* a horrible method of torture: With thick ropes, they beat me simultaneously in the neck, the back and the knees. Then they put needles under my fingernails and toenails

107

and they hit me with the "ox's cock," a type of whip used by the soldiers.

When I would lose consciousness, they would revive me with buckets of water. They also beat the soles of my feet with wooden sandals. Then they freed me with the warning that the next time they would kill me. When the soldiers freed me, I ran to where [Che and his men] were to tell them that I hadn't failed them, that the tortures didn't make me speak.

Che

I don't know if David is in Cuba today or if he followed his old employers, who have already been expropriated by the Revolution, but at the time he was a man who felt the need for a change. Although he couldn't imagine that it would also affect him and his world, he understood that the need to make that change was urgent.

David Gómez

When Che wrote those words in his book, I was an officer of the presidential palace guard, and one night when he went there he saw me and recognized me and embraced me; as he was embracing me, he said, "It's very good that you're here, very good."

Promotion

Fidel Castro

He was with [the wounded] for several weeks, until some time later, with the wounded already healthy, the small group of men joined the main column, which had grown due to the number of weapons seized in that battle.

Luis Crespo

It was in Arroyo del Infierno. They said, "Here come some troops." Troops? And Che appeared. He went to Fidel. And he said, "Here are my troops." I believe they even had a battle. A battle. You had to see it. I tell you, the things that Che had with him... And then to tell Fidel here are my troops... He had picked up all kinds of things. One of [the troops] had a shotgun, another a machete, a bucket, a tin can. He went to Uvero and picked up all the old weapons they had thrown out there as unserviceable; with them he armed his "troops," and with those "troops" he engaged in combat. The group he brought with him was a ragged lot, a disaster. And there he was talking with Fidel, in Arroyo del Infierno, with his ragged troops.

Fidel Castro
When for the first time we organized a new column, a second column, the command of that column was given to Che. And he was made a commander; thus, Che was the second commander of our forces.

Che
The amount of vanity that we all have inside made me feel like the proudest man on earth that day. The symbol of my commission, a small star, together with one of the wristwatches they had sent us from Manzanillo, were given to me by Celia.

Fidel Castro
And he began to operate with his small new column, in positions not very far from where Column One was located.

Alejandro Oñate Cañete
Orestes Guerra, Walfrido Pérez and several others went with Che, and since Che is honest, intelligent and unassuming, we were very happy with him.

Che
We had to do something to justify that semi-independent life we would lead in the new zone in the region of El Hombrito we were supposed to move to, and we began to ponder future heroic feats.

Alejandro Oñate Cañete

We carried out an attack, and they killed Joel's cousin, Hermes Caldero. We began the attack at a little past four o'clock, and the shooting lasted until six.

Joel Iglesias

Our first confrontation took place at the Bueycito Mines. There were few soldiers there, but they were well protected with sandbags. We had one death there; the garrison was made up of thirteen to seventeen soldiers, and they had a Springfield, a Garand and a .30-caliber machine gun. That was our first heavy weapon.

Che

I ordered him to stop, and the man holding the Garand made a motion. For me it was enough: I pulled the trigger with the intention of unloading the magazine of my machine gun into his body. However, the first bullet jammed and I was left defenseless. In the midst of a shower of bullets from the soldier's Garand, I ran with a speed that I have never again attained; flying in the air, I turned a corner and made it to the cross street, where I repaired the machine gun. The soldier, nevertheless, had inadvertently given the signal to attack, since his shots were the first to be fired. Hearing the shooting all around him, the soldier, frightened, hid behind a column; that's where we found him when the battle, which lasted only a few minutes, ended.

Joel Iglesias

Our operations spread throughout El Confín, El Hombrito, Marverde, La Mesa—that is, throughout the entire zone assigned to us by Fidel as our area of operations. We could leave the zone, but that was the center of our activity.

The Tooth-Puller

Joel Iglesias

One thing that gives an idea of what Che was like was the case of Maceo. Maceo, one of our *compañeros*, said he felt a vocation for nursing, so Che let Maceo give him injections twice a day so that he would learn and could later jab us. Che did this because when Maceo told us he wanted to give us injections, we all refused to be his guinea pig.

Che

On June 26, I had my debut as a dentist, although in the Sierra they gave me the more modest title of "tooth-puller." My first victim was Israel Pardo—today an army captain—who came out of it quite well. The second was Joel Iglesias. I tried just about everything short of putting a stick of dynamite in his mouth to get the tooth out, but my efforts were fruitless; he made it to the end of the war with the tooth in place. In addition to my lack of expertise, we had few anesthetics, so we had to use them very sparingly; thus I often tried psychological anesthetics, using some nasty epithets when people would complain too much about the work I was doing in their mouths.

Luis Alfonso Zayas

He pulled an awful lot of the *compañeros'* and the *campesinos'* teeth. For example, there's the case of a combatant who was later nicknamed The Patriot. Our resources were limited, and it appears that the *compañero's* tooth was so deeply rooted that Che ended up taking a hammer and a nailset and banging away. With each blow ·he asked, "Does it hurt?" And the man told him, "No." Those of us who were watching said that this man was a patriot, because there wasn't even any anesthetic.

111

The Slovenly One

Che

Crucito was a natural poet and he had long contests with Calixto Morales, a *Granma* expedition member and poet from the city. Calixto had given himself the nickname "nightingale of the fields," to which Crucito, in his peasant ballads, would answer disparagingly with the refrain, "You *guacaico* of the Sierra." [*Guacaica* is a bird found in Cuba of the cuckoo family, also known as *arriero;* its monotonous song is said to be similar to that used by the *campesinos* to herd animals.]

Calixto Morales

It was one of those nights that they sang that song. I don't know who composed it. It's sung to the music of "Francisco Alegre," and there's one part that goes like this: "Alas, Che Guevara, my commander / has a Browning / that he never cleans / the very slovenly one." And when the boys sing it, he laughs and laughs and laughs.

Che

[Frank País] gave us a silent lesson about order and discipline by cleaning our dirty guns, counting our bullets and putting them in order so they wouldn't get lost. From that day on I resolved to take better care of my weapon—and I succeeded, although I can't say that I was ever a model of meticulousness.

Duty

Calixto Morales

For him, fighting is nothing more than one part of our work. After the shooting is over, even if we've won, we must continue to work. We've got to count the casualties, write the communique on the battle and make an inventory of the material acquired. All of that. No meetings. No parties. Perhaps several days later, on any given night, we would meet to speak. He would take the opportunity to point out our errors, to say what had been done poorly, to analyze in detail what happened.

Joel Iglesias
Whether or not a battle was successful, he was in the habit of being the last one to withdraw. He would wait for the army to draw close and he might shoot at them or simply leave; he did this to protect his men even more. Later we convinced him to let one of the fighters under his command stay by his side.

Calixto Morales
He's the person who is least attached to life. He's always saying to me, "What will happen if they kill Che? Absolutely nothing."

Alejandro Oñate Cañete
We stopped on a hill I don't know the name of and we camped there for three or four days. We didn't fight at all until Camilo set an ambush to see if the army would fall into it, and the battle known as Marverde occurred. There they killed Ciro Redondo and wounded Joel.

Joel Iglesias
We had moved forward just a few meters—ten or fifteen— when they opened fire and hit me. Since I was ahead of my *compañeros,* I fell in no-man's-land and no one was able to help me. The *compañeros* took cover and began to fire at the soldiers to protect me.

Che
The *compañeros* told me that Joel was seriously wounded. All in all, Joel was extraordinarily lucky. They shot at him at pointblank range with three Garand rifles. Two bullets passed through his

own Garand and its butt was broken; another bullet hit him in the
hand, the next in the cheek, two went through his arm, two in one
leg and a few others grazed him as well. He was covered with
blood, but his wounds were nevertheless relatively minor.

Joel Iglesias

When he heard them shout out "They hit Joel," Che walked
over and bent down over me. He examined my wounds, he
touched me in silence and threw me over his shoulders.

Che

We got him out of there immediately and sent him on a
hammock to be treated at a hospital.

Joel Iglesias

When the soldiers were captured, they said they had seen
Che and recognized him, but they were so impressed, seeing
him come before them, standing on his feet, that they couldn't
shoot at him.

Che

The guerrilla fighter should never, under any circumstances,
leave a wounded *compañero* at the mercy of the enemy troops,
because the wounded man's fate will, almost certainly, be death.

Ambush

Alejandro Oñate Cañete

At a few minutes past one, they decided to head uphill, and
we set our ambush.

Che

We heard the troops shouting; they were involved in a very
violent argument. I was outside the wall, observing them, and I

personally was able to pick up the voice of the person in charge, apparently an officer, who was screaming, "You go in front, *por mis cojones!*" [because I say so; literally, "by my balls"] while the soldier, or whoever he was, answered angrily that he wouldn't. The discussion ended, and the troops began to move.

Alejandro Oñate Cañete

We passed the word down along the alley. Che ordered a *compañero* and me to place ourselves in front. He lay down near us, next to a felled tree trunk, with his automatic carbine.

Che

I was posted about twenty meters away, at an angle, behind a trunk that protected half my body, and aiming directly at the entry point of the road by which the soldiers were coming.

Alejandro Oñate Cañete

My other compañero opened fire as soon as he saw the soldiers, without waiting for the signal, and a firefight, which lasted about an hour or an hour and a half, began.

Che

Afterwards I found out it wasn't Camilo who fired; Ibrahím, nervous from the wait, fired too early, and in a few instants the shooting was widespread. A few minutes later—five or six—we felt the first mortars or bazookas fired by the soldiers whistling over our heads, but they passed by, exploding to our rear.

Alejandro Oñate Cañete

I'm behind a tree from which I have a view of the whole street and I see two guardsmen set up a bazooka and begin to fire.

Che

Suddenly I felt an unpleasant sensation—something like a burn or one's foot falling asleep—a sign that I had been hit in my left foot, which wasn't protected by the trunk. At the same time

115

I was wounded, I heard the clamor of people advancing toward me rapidly, precipitately, breaking branches on the way. My rifle was of no use, since I had just fired, and while lying on the ground, my pistol had gotten away from me. It was underneath my body, and I couldn't raise myself up because I was under direct enemy fire. With the quickness of desperation, I twisted and turned and managed to grab hold of the pistol.

Alejandro Oñate Cañete
I leave my position; I shoot and move backwards, running toward Che. When I'm close to him, the magazine of my Garand is already empty. I take it out to change it and I see Che, wounded on the ground.

Che
On top of the anguish I felt and the pain from the wound, suddenly came poor Cantinflas, telling me that he was retreating because his rifle was jammed.

Alejandro Oñate Cañete
I say to him, "Listen, this thing jammed."

Che
While he crouched at my side, I violently took the Garand from his hands and examined it; it was just the clip that was slightly out of line that had made it jam. I fixed it for him, with this cutting diagnosis: "What you are is a fool." Cantinflas—Oñate was his last name—took the gun and rejoined the battle, leaving the shelter of the trunk to empty his Garand in a demonstration of valor.

Alejandro Oñate Cañete
I was so furious he said that to me that I stood there on my feet, shooting.

116

Che

He couldn't empty it completely because a bullet, following a curious trajectory, penetrated his left arm and went out through his shoulder blade. Now the two of us were wounded.

Rigidity and Equality

Joel Iglesias

He was rigid as far as discipline was concerned: one example of that was when we set up camp between Marverde and Loma del Cojo. I gave out the assignments for sentry duty—a pair of men for every two hours—but I forgot to tell one pair who was going to relieve them. When their time was up, their replacements didn't show up, and they ended up doing four hours of guard duty. In the morning they told Che, since they considered it a breach of practice, and he summoned me and asked me about it. I told him that it seemed to me that they should have known who was going to relieve them. "That's your responsibility," he answered. "You're the chief, you organized the guard duty and you should have made sure it would go smoothly. So for the next night, do three extra hours." I did five hours of sentry duty for my irresponsibility.

Evelio Lafferté

He was very rigorous regarding the question of equality. If there was a box of cigars, it was for everyone there. I remember he had a series of tastes, so to speak, like preferring coffee without a grain of sugar. He also drank maté from a metal straw they sent to the Sierra for him. The majority didn't share his tastes, but he didn't mind if someone would take some of his maté or unsweetened coffee. I smoked a pipe and I would use his pipe tobacco. Moreover, since I was an asthmatic like him—although I wasn't as seriously afflicted—he gave me an atomizer

I still have, and when he received the Disné Inhal [inhaler], he shared it with me.

Harry Villega Tamayo (known as "Pombo" in Bolivia)

Che was a tough person, but along with that attitude he showed a great sense of humanity, a certain degree of paternalism toward us. He personally punished me on quite a few occasions. One time, because it occurred to me to shoot at a bush, he made me go three days without eating. On the second day of my punishment, he took me to a meeting, and at the end we all sat down at a table to eat. I asked the *campesinos* to intervene on my behalf so that my punishment would be lifted. One *campesino* asked Che why, if I was seated at the table, I wasn't eating; he answered that my mouth was the same as everyone else's, and added, "We don't stop him from eating; he can eat. He knows he's been punished; we leave to his judgment and his conscience to decide what his duty is." On that occasion, I couldn't eat.

Evelio Lafferté

He was extremely careful about sharing things. One night we were drenched by the rain, and Gallego from Minas del Infierno prepared the meal. I believe he had a turkey; he took the legs, the wings and the giblets and made a soup, to which he added a little rice. For those he called the officers, he prepared a fricassee.

"What are you making, Gallego?" Che asked him. "Soup for the boys who got wet in the rain," answered the man. "And that fricassee?" asked Che. "It's for the officers," said Gallego.

Everyone knows what happened. He picked up the casserole with the fricassee and dumped it all into the soup pot, and he uttered two or three profanities to Gallego.

Luis Crespo

First just Fajardo and I were together. We were in the same squad and we slept with our hammocks next to one another because we had only one plastic sheet. We shared everything. If we got a cigar, half for him and half for me. A cigarette, half and half. A can of milk, half and half. Then Che comes and says to us, "It would suit me to keep company with you since I eat a lot, but I don't eat a lot every day."

Fajardo and I always saved food, but Che had a different way of looking at things. He would say, "It's better to die with a full stomach than with an empty stomach." Then he would take the food and eat it right away, rapidly, wasting no time. Tomorrow? None of that. Tomorrow is another day. And whenever he got something, like a caramel, for example, he would immediately pick up a rock or a knife and cut it in three. He divided it in three pieces, one for each of us. Che was faithful to his friends, completely faithful. The people who were with him might have some complaints—it's highly unlikely someone would have no complaints—but he was very friendly, very respectful of others' opinions. The opinion of every person was something sacred to him. And when his men were right, he defended them. Without any sort of cliquishness, because he was categorical about that. Categorical.

Asthma

Che

Everyone could easily reach the crest and beyond, but for me it was a dreadful task. I made it, but I had such an asthma attack I could hardly take another step.

Luis Crespo

He had a deadly asthma attack.

Che

I remember the help the *guajiro* Crespo gave me. [*Guajiro* is a Cuban peasant.] When I could walk no longer and asked them to

119

leave me behind, the *guajiro*, with that vocabulary characteristic of our troops, said...

Luis Crespo

"You f____ing Argentine, son of a ____, walk, walk!" And he said, "No, leave me here, leave me." I took his pack and his gun and I carried him a while, and I kept on yelling at him.

Che

He was shouldering his own weight, the weight of my body and my pack, walking along difficult, hilly terrain with a deluge falling on our backs.

Luis Crespo

I pulled him up the hill, because he was in such bad shape he was dragging his feet. He dragged his feet uphill until on the other side we found the house of a *campesino* who was very kind to us. He stayed there with him.

Evelio Lafferté

Something that impressed me was his attitude toward his asthma. He would spend whole nights awake, and I would say to him, "How is it possible, given that you're a doctor, that you can't keep your asthma under control?" He explained to me the difficulties of treating asthma and the particular allergic complications in his case, as well as the requirements he would have to follow to attain at least some improvement; this would have meant granting him certain privileges as far as diet and the general regimen were concerned, which he felt would have been improper.

Víctor Bordón

We retreated at dawn. The path was hellish; Che was having an asthma attack and he had no more medicine to treat it; all the troops were tired, and he had to struggle just to stay on his feet.

On the way, we found several horses, and Che mounted one of them. A young combatant (who later died heroically) watched and voiced his criticism. Che listened to him, and he got off the horse and walked along with his column. The sun was rising when we reached the farm that was called El Cafetal.

We had begun to set up camp to rest when Che summoned me. His asthma attack hadn't let up. He ordered me to bring Soto, the young combatant. I had a premonition there would be a stormy discussion. When we got there, Che invited him to sit down. He spoke with Sotico for a long time; he explained to him why he had accepted the horse and said that he shouldn't see it as a privilege. "Are you convinced, lad?" he finally asked him, and he put his hand on the youth's shoulder. Sotico began to cry.

Education and Industry

Luis Crespo
He was very concerned about culture, about pronunciation, about how to say a word. He criticized me because I would say *cacbón* [instead of *carbón*]. These things like people speaking well mattered to him.

Che
We were able to lay the foundations for the first factories and permanent camps and put an end to our nomadic life. We carried out some operations of small significance, but our fundamental accomplishment was our evolution, at great hardship, to this more sedentary existence, carrying materials on our shoulders from very distant regions.

Luis Crespo
Another of his concerns was industrialization. Liberate a zone, become strong within it and then solve the food problem. He talked repeatedly about the importance of industrialization.

He was the one behind the first arms factory in the Sierra, the first shoe factory, garment shop, meat-curing shop, bakery, everything. He set up all kinds of things there.

Che

We were able to establish a shoe factory and a leather goods shop, an armory with an electric lathe, and a sheet metal and blacksmith's shop that was commissioned, among other things, to fill small brass grenades—an invention of ours, launched by rifle. They were fired with blanks and dubbed "the M-26." We also made ovens for baking bread, schools, auditing offices. Later we built installations for *Radio Rebelde* and published the first newspaper of the Cuban jungle, which we gave the same name as the Cuban rebel newspaper of the wars and 1868 and 1895: *El Cubano Libre* [The Free Cuban].

Luis Crespo

I don't know where he got hold of the mimeograph machine, but I do know that we received the newspaper. A messenger with Che's newspaper. I remember the first time: "Here comes Che's newspaper," they say, and I wonder, What are they talking about. Che's newspaper? But I see the pamphlet, that newspaper with a map of Cuba on the upper part, and I say to myself, it's true, Che's begun to write a newspaper. So the Sierra had its newspaper. Che published it. He would try to make sure that everyone read the press. If, for example, we received a copy of *Bohemia*, he would want everyone to read it. The same with any magazine or newspaper. He himself would see to it that we read the news.

Fidel Castro

I remember that Che took quite an interest in and put a lot of effort into creating *Radio Rebelde* at a time when we were just beginning to have a more or less stable territory at our disposal.

Thus, the first location of *Radio Rebelde* was near the camp Che had in the zone of La Mesa.

Che

When our first year of war had come to an end and we were beginning the second, we had a small transmitter.

Fidel Castro

I remember we were about 300 meters from the station and we tried to tune it in; it took us a lot of effort to get it.

Che

The first few formal broadcasts took place in February 1958, and the only listeners we had were Pelencho, a *campesino* whose hut was situated on the hill facing the station, and Fidel, who was visiting our camp.

Luis Crespo

When we got our radio transmitter, he made it his concern that everyone would be able to hear it, that it would reach the entire people of the countryside, that it would always be on the air. Not one part for the transmitter could be missing; everything had to work correctly. So that the radio would function smoothly, he himself dealt with everything within his power, any small, insignificant problem; he said that a simple thing now could become a big thing in the future. And what was put off for later, stayed that way. Everything had to be kept up to date.

Eduardo Fernández

The equipment we had was a Collins-brand transmitter, model 32-V-2. It's a medium-power piece of equipment; we managed to get one hundred twenty or one hundred thirty watts on the antenna. We used an Onan, one-kilowatt electric generator to power the transmitter, the record player and a light bulb they put there. Those were all the resources we had to begin our broadcasts.

Jorge Ricardo Masseti (Argentine journalist)

We were just about to finish our interview when four jet planes began to fly over the station, and we all ran to the air-raid shelter.

The spy plane from Cubana airlines continued flying in circles, as was habitual, while the four light planes sprayed shrapnel below each time they passed overhead.

"What a shame it is to lose this background sound!" I said, truly anguished, to Guevara.

"Isn't your tape recorder portable?"

"Yes."

"Then it doesn't matter whether the transmitter is working. Let's go!" he shouted, and he dragged me uphill until we entered the hut where the transmitter was located.

The planes continued firing; the sound of the motors and of the volleys of machine-gun fire was impressive.

I speeded up my questioning until I reached the point where I asked why the *campesinos* were being bombed. Just seconds after the attack ended, we began to broadcast the report.

But the risk we took was in vain. Interference on our frequency from Batista's intelligence service made our voices barely audible, and the explosions and the shooting were indistinguishable. Guevara laughed at my ill-fated attempt all morning.

The Triumph

Fidel Castro (address in Santiago)

Time is always an important factor. The revolution cannot be made in one day, but you can be sure that we are making the revolution. You can be sure that for the first time the Republic will truly be completely free and the people will have what they deserve. Power has not been the fruit of politics; it has been the fruit of the sacrifice of hundreds of thousands of our *compañeros*. Our only commitment is to the people and the nation of Cuba. A man is coming to power without commitments to any person; his exclusive commitment is to the people.

Nicolás Guillén (Cuban national poet)

One morning Leonidas Barletta, the editor of the well-read Buenos Aires weekly *Propósitos*, called at my hotel. "Guillén," he said. "I propose to you the following: We go to press this afternoon at a little past six, and we've decided, if it's possible, that you should send us a feature article or a poem in honor of Che Guevara, who at this time has so much prestige in your country. What do you think about an article or a sonnet? Whatever you decide upon, you'll have to hand it in a little past noon."

I was taken aback, and told him I couldn't do either because there wasn't enough time. A sonnet isn't written just like that; perhaps the feature. That's how we left it, and when I hung up...I began to write a sonnet.

I called Barletta almost at press time and I gave him these verses. Perhaps the readers are familiar with them:

As if San Martín hand of brother
to Martí pure had tended,
as if the River Plate had wended
to give the Cauto tenderness and water.

So Guevara, gaucho, voice of gall,
toasted Fidel with his guerrilla blood
and his broad hand was the most loved
when our night was the darkest night of all.

Death fled. Of its shadow stained
of beast, poison, dagger shoved
only the barbarous memory remains.

Two souls a single halo covers
as if San Martín had tended
to Martí hand of brothers.

Don Ernesto

I believe it was January 2d. I don't remember if I called Havana or Ernesto called Buenos Aires. In any case, as the connection was being made I could hear voices in English, voices with a Cuban accent and voices with a Buenos Aires accent. Finally a voice came through asking if he had the Guevara family. I answered that he did. I didn't recognize the voice. Then he says to me, "Well it's you, old man, your voice is unrecognizable." "You're the one that's unrecognizable. You're not speaking in Argentine anymore," I responded, and we began to talk. The whole family spoke with him.

Nicolás Guillén

The next day Barletta called me once more, happy like a child. He told me that the U.S. press agency Associated Press had given great political importance to the poem, distributing it from Buenos Aires to Mexico, in other words, throughout their whole Latin American network. I found out later that they picked it up to demonstrate the Communist influence in Cuba, since it was a Cuban of that political current who had written the passionate work praising the great Argentine guerrilla, who, besides, was an intimate friend of the leader of the revolution, Fidel Castro.

Editor

Among other articles adapted from the 1940 constitution in the Basic Law of the Republic of Cuba, proclaimed by the revolutionary government on February 7, 1959, was number 12 of Chapter 2, "About Nationality." In this article, a clause was added under the heading reading, "Those considered Cubans by birth include...":

e) foreigners who joined the armed struggle against the tyranny overthrown on December 31, 1958, serving two years or more in the Rebel Army and holding the rank of Commander for at least one year, as long as these conditions are certified in the manner prescribed by law.

This clause applied to only one man. Historically, one other revolutionary, Máximo Gómez, a Dominican, had received a similar distinction at the end of the conflict of 1895.

Che
To me, "Che" represents what's most important, what I'm most fond of in my life. How could I not like it? Everything that comes before, my first name and surname, are small, personal, insignificant. On the contrary, I like very much to be called Che.

Nicolás Guillén
During the last days of my stay in Buenos Aires to which I just referred, I visited Che's house, or rather, his family's house. It was then that I met Celia de la Serna, his mother, a very dynamic and very intelligent *compañera,* whose death surprised me as much as it caused me grief, since I had always seen her as having a seemingly inexhaustible vitality. Che's family's house was at 2208 Arenales Street; I ate the midday meal there twice, at the family's invitation.

Reunions

Don Ernesto
Several rebel officers met us and brought us directly to a room in the airport where we found Ernesto, surrounded by several soldiers.

We hadn't seen him for six years. My wife couldn't bear it and she began to cry as she embraced him. He was very thin and his hair fell to his shoulders. He had a big beard and dressed in a simple rebel military uniform. His arm was in a sling secured with a black silk kerchief. We mingled in a succession of emotional embraces. I remember Ernesto, in particular, stroking Juan Martín, who was ten years old when Ernesto left Buenos Aires; now he was a young man.

Fernando Barral (childhood friend)
I was a refugee in Hungary in 1960 after being freed from prison, and I read that the Hungarian press had written something about a revolutionary named Guevara, without giving his first name, who was an Argentine and a doctor. That's what they published, among other things. I didn't know he was a doctor, because I hadn't seen him since 1946. Later, at an international conference in Vietnam, I realized after speaking with the Cuban delegates that Guevara the guerrilla was my childhood friend. I mentioned it to a Chilean journalist, who told Che in Prague.

A little while later, Che passed through Hungary and he looked for me through his interpreter. He was in Hungary only a few hours and was very busy, and he couldn't find me.

When I learned that he was coming I also tried to see him, without any luck. But he left me a note, which he wrote on his place card during a meal held in his honor.

Che
I know you had some doubts about my identity but you believed that I was who I am, although, in effect, I'm not, because a lot of water has passed under my bridges; of the asthmatic and individualist you knew only the asthma remains. I learned that you have married; so have I. I have two children, but I am still an adventurer, only now my adventures have a just goal. Greetings to your family from this survivor from a time

gone by, and receive an embrace from Che, which is my new name.

Fernando Barral

After that, I wrote him telling him of my enthusiasm over the genuineness of the Cuban revoluton, about the number of dogmas it had disproved by its triumph alone, and saying that I wanted to come. I received an answer.

Che

It is truly a pity that we weren't able to see each other, if only for a few minutes. I write with the haste and accommodation that my many and diverse occupations demand of me.

I hope you understand. Concretely, although you don't say it in your last letter but in the previous one, it sounds like you would like to come work here. I can tell you right now that you have a job for yourself and your wife; that the pay will be respectable without permitting any great luxury; and that the experience of the Cuban revolution is something that seems to me to be very interesting for persons such as yourself who some day must begin anew in your country of origin. Of course you are welcome to bring your mother, and we would procure all the personal facilities you need for your work. The university is being reorganized and there is work there if you are interested. Naturally, you'll find more irrational things here than where you are now, since a revolution stirs everything up, upsets everything and little by little everyone has to be put in the position he is best able to perform. The only important thing is that no one's work be hindered.

To sum up, you're welcome here; if you want to come, let me know by whatever means you feel is best, and explain to me what procedures, if any, are necessary to bring your wife.

Since we have followed different paths for many years, let me tell you as far as my personal life is concerned that I am married, I have two children and I have received some news about our old

129

friends through my mother who visited us several months ago. Receive a fraternal embrace from your friend.

Fernando Barral

And I came here. I saw him at night at the Latin American Stadium where there was a soccer match with a Soviet team. When I saw that he was there, I approached him; he got up and greeted me, embraced me, let me sit by his side for the rest of the game and then he asked me to go with him to the ministry. We left by car with him driving, and he turned down the wrong streets, in the midst of a multitude of people screaming—"Che! Che!" —grabbing his hand, his clothes and smiling good-naturedly at him throughout. We arrived at the Ministry of Industries, and I was there for a rather short time.

He told me several things on that first occasion, but there was one thing he emphasized the most. Because I mentioned to him the satisfaction I felt seeing the atmosphere, the originality, the freshness, the anti-dogmatism, the dogmas the revolution broke with—the same things he had told me in the letter—he spoke to me clearly, he talked in more detail about all these things. One of the things he told me was that above all this was due to the fact that Fidel was a truly extraordinary man, and that this was one of the basic reasons for the triumph of the revolution and for the revolution being the way it was.

Alberto Granados

After saying farewell in Venezuela, I didn't see him again. I learned about the expedition and the landing, and after the triumph, we renewed our friendship.

Che

Mial: Your letter was no less pleasing for the fact that I was expecting it. I didn't write you inviting you to come to my new homeland because I was expecting to go to Venezuela with Fidel. Subsequent events prevented me from doing so. I thought I would go a little later, but ill health has kept me in bed. I hope to be able to go within approximately one month. I have been thinking about you so much that when they invited me to visit Venezuela, I demanded that I be given a few free days to spend them with you. I hope this wish soon becomes a reality. I won't respond to the cheap philosophy in your letter; for that we'll need a couple of matés, an *empanadita* and some corner under the shade of a tree: We'll talk there. Receive the strongest embrace that your macho dignity lets you accept from one of the same kind. Che.

Editor

Political circumstances stopped him from visiting Venezuela as he had planned in March 1959. It was Alberto who made the trip to Cuba.

Alberto Granados

What a question! What did I find the same and what did I find different in him?

He seemed a little huskier and perhaps taller; with the beard and olive-green uniform, he looked older, prematurely aged. That's what was different.

His voice had the same deliberate and ironic tone; he had the same reflective manner that I had known in him; the absence of conventionality, that character trait that I had criticized him for—for instance, the time he gave the straight truth to Pesce with no consideration of our debt of gratitude to him—had become more pronounced. Those stubborn characteristics of his that make you admire him totally or hate him, but don't allow indifference, were still there. Of course, I still called him Pelao and he continued with his Mial, to the astonishment of his assistant.

Don Ernesto

We were in a room at the Habana Libre Hotel on January 10, 1959. I spoke alone with Ernesto, and among other things, I asked him what he planned to do with "his" medicine. He stared at me and said, "My medicine? It's all yours. Since you have the same name as me you can put a plaque in your office and begin to kill healthy people." He laughed at his remark, but in a serious tone he quickly explained, "I'm not going to practice medicine any more. I know neither when nor on what land I'll end up."

President of the National Bank

Document

Decree number 2261

In use of the powers invested in me, and acting upon the nomination made by the Treasury and seconded by the Cabinet I move:

That Commander Ernesto Guevara Serna be named to fill the office of the president of the National Bank of Cuba.

The Minister of the Treasury will be responsible for carrying out this order.

Ratified in the Presidential Palace, in Havana, on November 26, 1959, Year of Liberation.

Osvaldo Dorticós
President

Fidel Castro Ruz
Prime Minister

Rufo López Fresquet
Minister of the Treasury

Raúl León Torres (Cuban economist)

The first appointment that Che, as president of the National Bank, had requested with me was scheduled for three o'clock. I showed up at that time, and Aleida told me I was mistaken, that the appointment was in fact scheduled for three, but three in the morning. And we met from three to four that morning.

That was in November 1959; it can be said with certainty that with Che as president, the revolution had come to the Bank, eleven months after the triumph.

The day after he assumed office he issued very precise regulations: documentation needed to authorize reimbursement for imported merchandise, financial operations payable in foreign currency, the sale of hard currency for foreign currency accounts, import licenses, purchase and sale of items valued in foreign currency, import and export of currency and securities, sale of dollars to tourists and other matters.

With these first measures he outlined certain concrete objectives: to implement policies aimed at stemming the flight of hard currency, limiting the amount of credit available to the private sector and supporting the agrarian reform program.

Those first few months were very intense. A number of measures were taken, such as the change of currency that took place in August 1961. Bilateral agreements were signed with socialist countries and the underdeveloped world. There was an effort both to find new markets for our sugar and new sources for imports.

One should keep in mind that the Bank was a bourgeois institution. Representatives of both Cuban and foreign commercial banks, holding completely different philosophical points of view from the Bank's president, sat on its board of directors.

There were very capable persons working there, highly qualified and experienced professionals; but they had bourgeois habits. In this area, Che was everyone's teacher, with his respect and his intransigence. A significant number of those professionals are still working for the Bank.

Che
Our most important task at that time was protecting our foreign currency reserves.

Document

I, ERNESTO GUEVARA SERNA, Cuban citizen, of legal age, married and resident of this Capital, named by Presidential Decree dated the twenty-sixth of November of nineteen hundred and fifty-nine to fill the position of President of the National Bank of Cuba, solemnly swear to fulfill my duties under the Basic Law and other Laws of Revolutionary Cuba, to uphold and defend them against all foreign or domestic enemies and to behave honestly and democratically.

Havana, the twenty-sixth of November of nineteen hundred and fifty-nine, Year of Liberation.

Che Ernesto Guevara

Eliseo de la Campa

It's already late afternoon when we land at the airport in Bayamo. He was on an official trip and had with him a guest and *compañera* Aleida, his wife. Shortly before nightfall the Commander orders me to get ready to leave for Havana, and I explain to him that the single-motor plane is in no shape to fly because the weather is bad. "I need to go to Havana," he insists, and we leave for Havana.

When we're flying above Manzanillo there's a threat of squalls. I tell him how the weather is pretty bad, and he orders me to return to Bayamo.

It's pitch dark in Bayamo, and there's no light there. So we begin to circle above the airport until the *compañeros* below can locate some kerosene lamps and put them in place, to illuminate the runway. These were the conditions in which we landed.

The thing is that Che doesn't leave the airport, he stays there, seated, as if he were going to wait the whole night for the weather to improve. Aleida approaches me and asks, "Eliseo, do you have any money?" And I did. "Listen," she tells me, "the problem is that Che doesn't have enough money even to pay for a hotel or to eat, he doesn't have anything and he was too embarrassed to ask you to lend him some." I told her there wasn't any problem, that I would pay for everything and we could settle up in Havana.

This was in the beginning of the revolution. The hardest thing for people to believe when I tell them this story is that Che was the president of the National Bank at the time, and the president of the Bank didn't have a single cent in his pocket.

The Chess Player

Enrique Oltuski (underground fighter)

He would come to the Central Planning Board office in the evenings, and after exhausting meetings he would play a chess match with his guards, while we would gather around and he'd sing the old tangos of his childhood in a low voice, very out of tune.

Eleazar Jiménez (international grandmaster)

He's such a simple man that you play a match with him without noticing that you're playing a leader of his caliber. He likes chess very much. I remember that in 1964, at the time of the sugar cane harvest, he's working the cane-cutting machines in Morón. We're in Camagüey with the Mexican team for a simultaneous display against players from the whole province. It's scheduled to start at 8:30 p.m., but we linger a bit at our meal and arrive at the tournament site at nine. Che is waiting at the door.

Che

This is the time you come? I traveled one hundred forty kilometers and I managed to get here on time, but you, who were here, made everyone wait half an hour.

Eleazar Jiménez

That night he defeats Armando Acevedo, the Mexican champion, in a brilliant match.

135

Emilio Carnero (Ministry of Industries official)

I play the last match with him. We tie. I want to keep a memento of him, so I ask him for the notation sheet. I want to show it to my grandchildren, I tell him. He laughs.

Che

Then I'm going to write that it was a draw so you don't tell them that you beat me.

The Chronicler

Félix C. (combatant in the Sierra)

Just imagine the number of things we went through together in the war, and when he decides to write something, look at what he remembers, see what caught his attention!

Che

Given the difficult conditions in the Sierra Maestra, it was a glorious day. We were patiently following the troops of Sánchez Mosquera along Agua Revés, one of the steepest and most intricate valleys of the Turquino River basin. That obstinate assassin left a trail of burned huts and indignant sadness throughout the region, but his path would inevitably lead him to climb to one of the two or three points of the Sierra where Camilo was supposed to be waiting for him. It could be the Nevada Summit, or it could be what we called "Cripple's Summit," now known as "Dead Man's Summit."

Camilo had left in a hurry with around twelve men, part of his vanguard group, and that small number of fighters had to be divided among three locations to stop a column of a little over one hundred soldiers. My mission was to descend on Sánchez Mosquera from behind, encircling him. Our main concern was laying siege to him; thus we followed at a distance, and with great patience, as huts went up in flames set by the enemy rearguard. We were far away, but we could hear the cries of the

136

soliders. We didn't know how many of them there were in total. Our column was walking with difficulty along the hillsides, while the enemy marched along the bottom of the narrow valley.

Everything would have been perfect had it not been for our new mascot. He was a small hunting dog, just a couple of weeks old. Although Félix had repeatedly admonished him, telling him to go back to our center of operations—a house where the cooks stayed—the puppy followed our column. Because there are no trails in that part of the Sierra Maestra, hiking on the slopes is very hard. We crossed a difficult *"pelúa"*—a place where felled trees are covered by a new growth of vegetation, making the crossing arduous. We traipsed over trunks and thicket, trying not to lose contact with our guests.

The small column marched in silence, as is usual in these cases, not letting anything—even a broken stick—upset the habitual rustling of the forest. But suddenly the silence was broken by the sorrowful and nervous wails of the little dog. He had fallen behind and was barking desperately, calling on his masters to help him through the difficult stretch. Someone carried the animal across and we continued on our march. But when we were resting at the bottom of a river bed with a lookout watching the movements of the enemy army, the dog once again let loose his hysterical howls. He was no longer content with calling us; he was afraid we were going to leave him and he barked desperately.

I remember my categorical order: "Félix, that dog is not going to howl any longer; you take charge of doing it. Strangle him. He can't be allowed to bark again." Félix looked at me without any expression in his eyes. Amidst our tired troops, sort of in the center of a circle, were Félix and the little dog. With great deliberateness, he took out a piece of rope, fit it around the puppy's neck and began to tighten it. The affectionate movements of his tail soon became convulsive and slowly died away, along with an intent moan that eluded the unyielding noose around his neck. I don't know how long it was, but it seemed to all of us that a long time passed before the end finally arrived.

The puppy, after a last nervous twitch, stopped struggling. He stayed there, emaciated, his little head bent over some branches in the underbrush.

We continued marching without even mentioning the incident. Sánchez Mosquera's troops had gotten a way ahead of us, and a short while later we heard some shots. We headed quickly down the hillside over the difficult terrain, searching for the best path to catch up with the enemy rearguard; we knew that Camilo had taken action. It took us a long time to reach the last house before the land went up again. We moved very cautiously, expecting to find the enemy at any moment. The shooting had been heavy, but it didn't last very long; we were all tense in expectation.

The last house was also abandoned. There was no sign of the soldiers. Two scouts climbed "Cripple's Summit" and returned a short while later with the news: "There's a grave up there. We opened it and found a soldier buried there." They also brought the victim's papers, which they found in his shirt pocket. There had been a fight and one death. The death was theirs, but we knew nothing more.

Dejected, we slowly returned. Two scouting missions revealed clear trails of footprints on both sides of the Maestra Summit, but nothing else. The return trip, this time by the path in the valley, went slowly.

At night we came upon a house, also empty; it was in the hamlet of Mar Verde, and we were able to rest there. They quickly cooked a pig and some yuccas, and in a short time the meal was ready. Someone sang a tune, with a guitar; the houses of the *campesinos* had been abandoned with all their belongings inside.

I don't know if it was because the song was sentimental, or if it was the night or the fatigue. In any case, Félix, who was sitting on the ground eating, threw a bone down. The dog of the house meekly came and picked it up. Félix put his hand on its head. The dog looked at him; Félix looked back, and we exchanged a sort of a guilty look. Suddenly we all fell silent. There was an imperceptible emotional sensation that passed among us. There with us all, with his meek, impish look and a hint of reproach, observing us through another dog, was the murdered puppy.

The October Crisis

Joaquín Ross *(campesino)*

In January 1959, we're building a tourist center in La Güira, and it occurs to me to tell Carlos Fernández, the engineer, that near San Andrés de Caiguanabo there's a cave they call Los Portales that's a wonderful attraction for those who enjoy nature, and the engineer becomes enthusiastic about the place and he tells me to get to work and asks how many workers I need.

Right away I think that the *campesinos* from the area are the right ones since they need the work to live, and I start out with twenty-one of them and later they raise the number of men to one hundred and we pick up thirty more to put down a little road to La Güira and a little while later more personnel began to come and all of them want to visit the cave and how wonderful and how beautiful it is with its river passing through the stone arches and its deep hollows and beautiful views.

Among the personnel who came from afar to see Los Portales was a commander, and he loved the cave and began to come very often and to speak with me and ask me things about the place, about the bushes I brought and planted, about those the Forest Service brought.

He liked the stones, the place, the rustic things, the natural atmosphere, and one day he asks me, "What's the name of that tree up there?" It turns out that it was something that's not from around here that was recently planted and the little sign that said its name had been lost and I didn't remember the name on the sign, and I tell him that.

He began to laugh and he answers, "If you want, we'll name it 'Won't-Be-Forgotten.'" And that's the way we left it, and who

139

could forget such a name? So that's how he would come, take a little walk around the place and leave.

Around the year of 61, he sent Avelino González to be the director, and the man came to see me and I told him what I needed. With him the highway was built, lights were put in and all that. Then the captain of the zone said that it was military, a military zone, and that civilians couldn't be there, and they sent me to another area, they moved my little house at the foot of the cave and I went to work in another place.

The commander came back and ordered them to find me, they put a military telephone in my house since it was so far from civilization, they gave me a FAL rifle. On October 21st or 22nd, they come to look for me at my house, and I go out the back way until I reach the toilet, thinking I'll make a circle and surprise them from behind, because I don't know who they are and I have heard that things are going very poorly and all around the cave I see little lights that are nothing but trucks, many trucks and the soldiers who were looking for me bring me to Captain Méndez Sierra. The captain asks me if there is electricity in the zone. I tell him yes, but there are no light bulbs. He asks me if I can get hold of some to light up the cave, and I leave for the hamlet and I take all the bulbs from the houses, and in this way the cave was lit. The next day they got more light bulbs, and I went around the hamlet again putting the bulbs in.

And the same commander who would come to visit the cave and spend hours looking at the caves is the chief of all those men and he goes around with his olive green shirt hanging outside his pants and his belt over it, a cigar burning and his arms on his hips, walking from one place to another.

"Do you have a uniform?"

"No."

"Let Supplies give you a complete outfit."

When they gave me the clothes, I was on my way home and halfway there I was already taking off a boot, taking out the shirt, and before I had gotten twenty-five meters further, I was already in uniform.

I knew where each well in the cave was, where you could find each thing you were looking for. He would come to my house and my wife would cook for a group of them. One time he came and there was *chicharrón* [crisp pork rinds or cracklings] and *malanga* [an edible root], but he would never accept something if there wasn't enough for all.

Listen to me, I wish a third of this nation could have known him as I did! You know, each time I go to the cave, when I walk through it, it seems to me that I see him coming down some of its steps with his hands on his hips, smiling with his eyes, and with the smoke of his cigar covering part of his face.

With him, there in the headquarters, was his general staff. If you've been in the cave, you can see the place where he slept. They put three cinder-block walls in front of one little cave, and in that cave he had a cot. With the humidity in there and him with his asthma, I asked him how could he sleep like that, and he answered that it agreed with him, that the heat was good for his asthma.

That whole place was filled with military trenches you could walk along without being seen, and he liked walking around all those places. One time he told me that it reminded him of the Sierra Maestra; I've never been there, but around here things are pretty complicated.

Look, for you to be a *guajiro* and find yourself with a man who treats you like he treated men, I, who before had no future and worked other people's land... Today, today I am Don Joaquín. Before I wasn't even Joaquín.

Nobody could get Che to drink sweetened coffee; he had his habits. Listen, one time we were in the mess hall and they serve black-eyed peas, but they bring him white rice, pared pineapple and marmalade. I've never seen a man angrier. He threw the plate down so hard that the sparks reached the river and then he chewed out the cook in such a way that I thought he was going to kill him, Che was so angry.

That's the way he was; those are men who add and add and don't subtract. He was one of those who have three plus five plus seven. Because there are some around who are seven minus five minus three.

Little by little we are restoring this place that was his camp and today is a national monument; I don't want it to be missing anything. Look, he hung his hammock between a *jocuma* tree and a *baría* tree. The *jocuma* split in two and people wanted to plant another one, but what I did was to look for the shoot from the same plant because it's unlikely that another *jocuma* like that one would grow in stone.

He was honest, a complete man. I love that cave a lot, because, as I say, I see him coming down some of its steps, calm, at a slow pace, with his short beard and his chewed-up cigar between his lips, with his arms on his hips and his smiling eyes.

Ministry of Industries

Document

Decree number 2950

Presidency

In use of the powers invested in me

I move:

To appoint Dr. Ernesto Guevara de la Serna, commander, as Minister of Industries.
Ratified in the Presidential Palace, in Havana, on February 27, 1961.

Osvaldo Dorticós
President

Che

Quality should be one of the factors used to evaluate our efforts. If today some products have changed in appearance or taste, in the future we shall find the proper formulas, the necessary ingredients. As we move forward, we should take into consideration the importance of quality for the well-being of the population, and not sacrifice it as we increase production.

Franciso Hernández (technician of the former Coca-Cola plant)

The first question he asked me was if I was the technician of that department, and when I answered affirmatively, he continued his questioning to find out what we were doing to substitute imports. We were struggling to find a syrup that would match the flavor of Coca-Cola. I showed him some of the vats holding the test syrups. With a movement of his hand he indicated that things weren't going well.

"What are you doing to solve this problem?" he asked me, and I explained to him that I hadn't slept for a number of nights trying to find that blessed substitute, but we didn't have the basic ingredients. "It must be found, no?" he said. I told him we would produce it.

Subsequently he made several visits, and he also suggested that the factory producing extracts and concentrates should become independent, so it could supply other soft-drink producers. He consulted with us about this, he asked the personnel what they thought, and when we were all in agreement, he himself gave us the address of a building where, from that point on, the production unit has been located.

One day in a talk I saw Che giving on television, he said that the soft drink tasted like cough syrup. It hurt me a lot; I felt offended because I was doing everything I could, and at the first chance I had, I let him know. He responded:

"We have to be honest and always tell the truth. We shouldn't only speak about what's good, but also criticize what's bad."

"But if we've improved the taste, Commander..."

"That's not enough. It's our duty to give the people the best, and you shouldn't feel offended because you're part of the people; I'm sure you'll continue your efforts to achieve a product of maximum quality."

Time went by, and we continued experimenting. One day I was surprised to hear his voice calling my name. He had recognized me there in the middle of the street, and said to me, simply, "Congratulations, Pancho. The flavor has improved one hundred percent."

Che

Remember that work is the thing that is most important. Excuse me if I insist on this again and again, but the truth is that without work there is nothing. All the wealth of the world, all the things of value possessed by humanity, are nothing more than accumulated work. Without this, nothing can exist.

Alcides Bedoya

Every two months, in meetings with the managers of enterprises, he would sometimes speak about art, or music or international politics. One day he's asked to talk about ethics. "It's the most difficult subject you've asked me to address," he says. No one missed these meetings because in addition to subjects related to our work, he touched upon many other things.

Arturo Guzmán

Every month he makes an analysis of the total production of the ministry. The meeting takes up a Sunday from two in the afternoon until midnight. He asks questions ranging from management to the product in order to have detailed knowledge of what's happening.

Alcides Bedoya

He makes an analysis of each individual enterprise; he listens to what the managing board has to say and then he draws conclusions. The way he combines the smallest details of any activity with a broad vision of technical-economic development in a given branch of production is really remarkable. He gives directives for development looking twenty years into the future. He never asks how things are going; he already knows that. He speaks about concrete aspects of things or about future prospects; he always leaves you with something new.

Arturo Guzmán

He subjects the ministry cadre to periodic tests in the meetings held to discuss and receive guidance on general problems. For this purpose, he sets a personal example. To promote voluntary work in the ministry, he steps forward beginning on day one.

Alcides Bedoya

The "Communist Work Bonds" were his idea. He believes that voluntary work not only increases production, but that it is essential for people's development.

Arturo Guzmán

He also introduced the "Demotion Plan," which consists of making managers at all levels work one month a year in positions of lower responsibility. He always places great importance on experience at the bottom, on practice. Almost all of the leadership cadre come from the factories, from the trial of work and life; for years this is his method of selecting cadre.

Alcides Bedoya

The factories have to be visited every two months; no excuse is good enough. He manages to make the visits, and no one has more work than he does.

Arturo Guzmán

His work day is the same: The lights in his office on the ninth floor are on until daybreak. He believes that if you work well you are simply fulfilling a duty. In any case, the reward is a more difficult task and greater responsibilities.

Alcides Bedoya

He's very stingy with praise. But despite the fact he's so strict, no one tries to hide anything from him; people say I made a mistake here, or there. Because at the same time, he inspires confidence; above and beyond discipline, he is more humane than anyone else in the ministry.

Rolando Baquero

One time we head out in several trucks to do voluntary work. He travels in the newest truck. When it's time to return, he's delayed a bit, and everybody gets in the same truck so they can travel with him. But he doesn't show up. On the road we see that he's aboard an old truck with just two or three other persons.

Osvaldo Rodríguez,

During the period in which he worked in the *Consolidado del Plástico*, there's a fire in the Aldabó warehouse. The firefighters don't let anyone in because of the threat of the building caving in, in addition to the toxic gases. He arrives and is the first one to enter, without a mask or anything. He spends four days there removing raw materials from the ruins.

Che

Yes, material incentives are the antithesis of the development of consciousness, but they are a great lever for improving production. Should it be understood that preferential attention to the development of consciousness slows down production? In comparative terms, in a given period of time, possibly, although no one has made the relevant calculations. We believe that in a relatively short time, the development of consciousness does more for development of production than material incentives, and we base this affirmation on our general vision of the development of society toward communism.

Arturo Guzmán

He suggests that the development of consciousness is the only possible route leading to the new society. He believes that socialism cannot develop a person using the spent weapons of capitalism; that material incentives are a necessary evil that must be eradicated definitively; that no person with consciousness can be replaced by persons motivated by material incentives. Looking at it from a historical perspective, the "new man" is already old in him; in his life, we can see the virtues he proclaims are necessary for that new social being.

5

*BENEATH MY LEGS I FEEL THE RIBS OF ROCINANTE**

Once gain I feel the ribs of Rosinante [sic]
beneath my legs; once more I hit the road with my shield
upon my arm.

> —from a letter by Che to his parents, mid-1965

Dear Hildita,

Although you'll receive this letter much later, I'm writing to you today because I want you to know that I remembered and I hope you're having a very happy birthday. You're a woman now and I can't write to you as if you were a child, telling you fibs and foolish things.

You should know that I'm still far away and will be far from you for a long time, doing what I can to struggle against our enemies. It's not such a big deal, but at least I'm doing something, and I hope you will always be able to be proud of your father, as I am of you.

Remember that there are still many years of struggle left and even when you're a grown woman you'll have to do your share in the struggle. Meanwhile, you have to get ready, be very

*Rocinante was the sorry mount of Cervantes' Don Quixote.

revolutionary—which at your age means to learn a lot, as much as possible, and always be ready to support just causes. Moreover, obey your mother and don't be too sure of yourself quite yet; you'll get there soon enough.

You should struggle to be one of the best in school, best in every sense. You know what this means; in your studies and revolutionary attitude; that is, good behavior, seriousness, loving the revolution, camaraderie, etc.

I wasn't like that when I was your age, but I lived in a different society where man was the enemy of man. You are privileged to live in another time and must show yourself worthy of it.

Don't forget to go by the house to check on the other kids and remind them to study and behave, especially Aleidita, who pays heed to you as her older sister.

Well, old girl, once again, have a very happy birthday. Give your mama and your cousin a hug, and to make up for all the time we won't see each other, receive a big, strong hug from your

PAPA

Points of View

Antonio Peredo (Bolivian guerrilla, brother of Inti and Coco)

Che's plan was essentially political. If you look at it from that point of view, I don't think it was a failure; it seems to me that throughout Bolivia people agree with this idea.

Che's arrival in Bolivia is related to a specific political situation. In the decade of the 50s, there was a long period of revolutionary nationalism, which came to an unhappy end in 1964. From that point on, a military dictatorship of the fascists took over and committed several massacres of the mine workers. Given this political context, Che sees Bolivia as a flash point of the Latin American situation and believes that from this point the revolutionary struggle can spread throughout a great part of the continent.

You have to remember that for Che—as he says in many of his writings and as any revolutionary would hold—guerrilla struggle is a method and what's important isn't the guerrillas in and of themselves, but the revolutionary struggle. As a form of revolutionary struggle then, even with its failure militarily—if you can call it that—Che's political struggle is a success because of its subsequent importance, not only in Bolivia, but in the rest of Latin America.

Che
We believe that the three fundamental contributions of the Cuban revolution to the mechanics of Latin American revolutionary movements are:

1. Popular forces can win a war against the army.
2. You don't always have to wait until all conditions for a revolution are present; the insurrectional *foco* [center of guerrilla operations] can create them.
3. In the underdeveloped areas of America, the principal arena of armed struggle should be the countryside.

Daniel Alarcón ("Benigno" in Bolivia)
We were there when several people asked him why he was giving up his rank, position and citizenship, his responsibilities as minister, etc. He began to explain, to give a series of explanations that convinced us to join him—even though we understood that as officers of the Revolutionary Armed Forces we could be compromising our country. We decided, like Che, that we had to give up our rank, positions and citizenship in order to create a completely uniform group.

Che's interest in the group's equality was apparent when we set up our training camp. Although guarding the camp wasn't really necessary, he spoke of the need to begin to do so, so that from the outset we'd rid ourselves of the habit of seeing

151

ourselves as officers and become soldiers instead. From then on, late at night, as soon as we finished our studies, we would begin guard duty.

For the first two or three days we tried to exclude him from guard duty. But when a few days had gone by and he hadn't been called to take his turn, he asked who was responsible for assigning the duty. The *compañero* San Luis said that he was; so then Che asked him why he had been left out. Knowing what Che was like, San Luis couldn't figure out how to answer him. Embarrassed, he said, "The truth is that I'm to blame; I was the one who didn't want to assign you." Then Che said to him, "You must give me an assignment; tonight I'm taking the first shift."

Roberto Peredo

Long before the guerrilla struggle was launched, there were discussions between the Communist Party leadership and Che, establishing in principle the conditions—political conditions, of course—under which the CP leadership would offer its support. More than anything else, the support hinged on the guerrilla force being made up largely of CP cadre. This, in fact, occurred, although it turned out that in order to join the guerrillas these cadres had to leave the CP.

Fidel Castro

Che had established relations with leaders and militants of the Bolivian Communist Party and asked them to support the movement in South America, before the split in the party occurred. Some of the militants worked with him for years on various tasks, with the authorization of the party. The split created a touchy situation, given that militants who had worked with him ended up in different factions.

Che, however, didn't conceive of the Bolivian struggle as an isolated event, but as part of a revolutionary movement of liberation that before long would spread to other South American countries. His purpose was to organize a movement devoid of sectarian spirit, which all those who wished to struggle for the liberation of Bolivia and the other nations in Latin America subjugated by imperialism could join. But in the initial phase of setting up the guerrilla base, he was dependent in a fundamental way on the aid of a group of brave and discreet collaborators who remained in Monje's party after the split.

Daniel Alarcón

In order to save time at target practice, we'd station two *compañeros* behind the rocks where the targets were placed so they could give us our marks from there. Che was never assigned this task because it was extremely dangerous. We tried to protect him whenever we could; but then he said that just as any one of us could be there, so could he, and that if we graded his shots, why shouldn't he grade ours.

Mario Monje (former general secretary of the Bolivian Communist Party)

I first met Che in 1962. We met with each other again a few times in 1963 and 1964. It seems important to me to mention my meeting with Che, and later with Fidel, in 1964. Che was one of those people who was convinced you couldn't wage guerrilla warfare in Bolivia; that's what he said in '64, recalling the time he spent in Bolivia around 1952. He didn't think a guerrilla force could win in Bolivia. He thought our country should try to understand; that is to say, that we should somehow wait for the revolution to succeed in other countries.

Antonio Peredo

In a broader sense, Che, as well as other guerrilla leaders, believed—and justly so—that support would come from broad sectors of the proletariat. This was unquestionably proved correct in Bolivia. Shortly after the guerrilla struggle began, in the month of June, mineworkers from three principal mining centers held a special assembly at which they agreed to provide "moral, material and physical support." These were the words they used in their public statement of support for the guerrillas.

How was this support shown? In an offer to send men and materials (you have to remember that the miners in Bolivia still had weapons as a result of the revolutionary struggle of 1950); and in money, through the donation of a day's wages from all the workers in the three centers (they numbered around 25,000 in total). This decision, this resolve of the miners, provoked an immediate reaction from the government. Something like ten days after the miners' assembly, on the night of a fiesta, the army pillaged these three mining centers and committed a massacre, leaving ninety dead, including women and children; this was the official figure, which many consider to be lower than the actual number killed. This massacre was tribute—paid in blood—from the mineworkers to the guerrilla struggle initiated by Che.

Daniel Alarcón

I still remember him saying goodbye to us with that phrase he would use: "Well, I'll see you there." About an hour before he left, he gathered us together and said: "Lads, it's not too late to change your mind. If any of you feels you aren't up to the task before us as we've defined it, you still have time to say so. We won't call you a coward, a traitor or anything like that. Naturally, every human being has the right to feel afraid, and anyone who doesn't, can't be a human being. Fear is natural; the fact is that we feel it, and I, in particular, have felt it, not once, but many times. But what you need is a clear conviction about why you are struggling; and what you must do, above all, is pull yourself together in order to overcome this fear, or at some other point it may overpower you. In other words, everyone feels fear, but if we really stick to our guns and continue on our course, we can overcome it.

"But there still may be someone who hasn't overcome it; if he isn't in the best shape to leave with us, it's not too late to say so. I, for one, will not call you a coward; but you should speak out here and now. We don't want anyone to play a sinister role out

154

there. We want to do the best we can, and in one way or another let this revolution feel the pride that she deserves."

At that point he said goodbye to us; inside his car, before leaving, he spoke to a *compañero*. "Listen," he said, "try to make sure that the *compañeros* go see their families and that this isn't for any reason neglected. Everything must be done as we've planned; as soon as the *compañeros* begin to arrive, they'll let me know who was able to carry out all his tasks and who, because they weren't given everything they needed on time, wasn't. Remember, the *compañeros* only have a few days left, and the plan must be carried out to the letter."

Mario Monje

In August 1966, it was suggested I meet with Che. I was happy to get the chance to talk with Che, but I told them it wasn't the right moment. In September, some misunderstandings arose between ourselves and the Cubans. The presence of [French writer Régis] Debray placed me in a somewhat uncomfortable situation. I'm very sensitive and I believed that Debray was part of a foreign phenomenon, that in reality certain existing relations were being violated. Previously, they had approached us in a different way, one that would have allowed our party to join the struggle.

Given this situation, the CP leadership decided to declare that the Bolivian revolution had to be led by Bolivians and that we believed Bolivians could solve their own problems. With this purpose in mind, I left Bolivia in early November.

I arrived in Havana in December and spoke with Fidel. In response to my position, Fidel asked me to meet with Che outside Bolivia. He indicated that Che wasn't in Bolivia and that the meeting could take place somewhere close to the border.

I returned to Bolivia on December 23rd or 24th, certain I would have to leave the country again to meet with Che. But I believed that Che was in Bolivia; a number of factors led me to believe that some rather murky things were going on. The meeting with Che, to a certain extent, helped me understand what was happening.

Fidel Castro

It was in deference to [the guerrilla collaborators who remained in Monje's party], in the first place, that he invited Monje to visit his camp, although he wasn't the least bit sympathetic toward him. He subsequently invited Moisés Guevara, a mineworkers' and political leader who had left the party to help form another organization, and then left the latter group in disagreement with its leader, Oscar Zamora. Zamora was another "Monje," who some time earlier had committed himself to working with Che to organize armed guerrilla struggle in Bolivia. Later, however, he reneged on his commitments, folding his arms in a cowardly manner when the moment for action arrived. After Che's death, Zamora, in the name of "Marxism-Leninism," became one of his most venomous critics. Moisés Guevara joined Che without vacillating, as he had promised long before Che arrived in Bolivia. He offered him his support and heroically gave his life to the revolutionary cause.

Che

AT 7:30, the doctor arrived with the news that Monje was there. I went with Inti, Tuma, Urbano and Arturo to meet him. The reception was cordial but tense; an unspoken question hung in the air: What have you come for?

The discussion with Monje began with generalities, but he soon got to the point. His fundamental position can be summarized in three basic conditions:

1. He would resign from the party leadership, but he would see to it that the party, at the least, remain neutral, and that cadres be taken from the party to join the struggle.

2. He would provide the political-military leadership of the struggle as long as the revolution was Bolivian in scope.

3. He would handle relations with other South American parties and try to persuade them to support the liberation movements (he mentioned [Venezuelan guerrilla leader] Douglas Bravo as an example).

Mario Monje

He began the conversation stating that he needed to clarify a few things so that the discussion of problems could be held in an atmosphere of frankness. Concretely, he said, "I'd like to apologize, we've deceived you; we couldn't explain our plans to you. I know you haven't been able to get along with the Cuban *compañero* who was here; he's more military- than political-minded. He couldn't tell you everything, but here we are, and this region is my liberated territory."

Then I stated very specifically that the Bolivian revolution must be led by Bolivians. I further suggested that a body or committee be created in which not only the CP but also other revolutionary forces would be represented; and I said that I believed there were people around who were capable of leading the revolution forward, and I was willing to work under their leadership.

But I didn't think they had the right attitude, considering the national and international questions that were at stake. They hadn't taken this situation into account. Their attitude was understandable; when we discussed the problem of leadership of the revolution, Che himself said he had a lot of experience, he had seen what happened in Peru in 1963, in Argentina in 1964, what happened in the Congo, and he believed they should be the ones to carry out, head or lead a revolution, that they couldn't place themselves under another force because they were in a position to go ahead with it. And he said they had chosen this country because they had made an evaluation of certain of its characteristics: a weak army, a reactionary government such as that of Barrientos, a weak bourgeoisie that could be defeated.

I explained to Che—as I had to Fidel a year earlier and had been repeating for a long time—our position on the Bolivian revolution. I suggested that what was needed was to build a party on a national scale, a military organizaton capable of carrying out a revolution in a time of crisis, once certain conditions existed.

Then he said to me, "I can't give you the leadership of the revolution because you don't believe in guerrilla struggle. You have different plans; you are preparing for, you believe in, an insurrection, in an uprising of a national character with no set date or time; you're waiting for the sharpening or the appearance of certain contradictions."

I told him yes, you understand me, that's what I think, because I don't believe a guerrilla struggle will lead to revolution.

So the conversation continued in a vicious circle; he continued arguing his points of view, and I mine, until he pointed out that in effect we couldn't reach an understanding, that we were talking about two different things. I told him I'm conscious of and very sincere about what I'm doing and saying; that sometimes one must take these positions bearing in mind the process that will ensue: If you triumph with the revolution, I'll end up in the trash bin of those who considered themselves to be revolutionaries, but at the decisive moment didn't know how to play their role. So I understand; I know of Kautsky, Bernstein, Trotsky, and I wouldn't be surprised if out of a lack of understanding of this country's situation that sort of case might arise. But even so, I believe I understand the Bolivian problem better than you.

Che

I answered that his first point was up to him as party secretary, although I considered his position to be a great mistake. It was vacillating and accommodating, and it would preserve the historical name of a group that should be denounced for its defeatist position. Time would prove me right.

Regarding the third point, I had no objections to him trying to do this, but he was doomed to failure. Asking Codovila [sic] to support Douglas Bravo was like asking him to condone an uprising inside his own party. [Douglas Bravo was a Venezuelan Communist and top commander of the Armed Forces of National Liberation (FALN). He came into conflict and eventually split with the Venezuelan Communist Party in the mid-1960s over the latter's suspension of support for armed struggle. Vittorio Codovilla was the longtime orthodox leader of the Argentine Communist Party.] Again, time would be the judge.

As for the second point, there was no way I could accept it. I was to be the military leader and I could not allow any ambiguity in this respect. The discussion bogged down over this issue, spinning around in a vicious circle.

Fidel Castro

The group of Bolivian guerrillas who had remained in Monje's organization up to that point also did their part. Led by Inti and Coco Peredo—who later proved to be brave and outstanding fighters—they left Monje and supported Che unequivocally.

Mario Monje

To protect a revolutionary who was passing through the country, I assigned several *compañeros* to collaborate with the Cuban *compañero* who was in the country. In addition, I agreed to let them communicate their experiences and use these contacts to recruit comrades from my party to work with them in accordance with their own political position.

Che

The way we left it was that he would think it over and speak with the Bolivian *compañeros*. We went to the new camp, and there he spoke with everyone, presenting them with the choice of either staying or supporting the party. Everyone chose to stay; it seems this was a blow to him.

At twelve o'clock, we drank a toast; he pointed out the historical importance of the date. I took advantage of his remarks to say that this moment marked the new "shout of Murillo" of the continental revolution [the "grito de Murillo" was the proclamation of independence from Spain by Pedro Domingo Murillo and his followers in La Paz in July 1809; their rebellion was crushed, and Murillo and eight of his fellow conspirators were executed in January 1810, but their movement was a forerunner of successful independence movements all over Latin America], and that relative to the actual fact of the revolution, our lives meant nothing.

Fidel Castro

But Monje, not satisfied with the outcome, tried to sabotage the movement, intercepting well-trained communist militants in La Paz who were going to join the guerrilla forces. These facts show how there are men within the revolutionary ranks who are endowed with all the necessary qualities to join the struggle, but whose development is criminally frustrated by incompetent, spurious and scheming leaders.

Guerrilla Number Six (unidentified)

I'm number six of the first Bolivian group that trained for guerrilla struggle in Bolivia in 1966. There were nine of us, all Bolivians, and the group was led by Mario Monje, at the time first secretary of the Bolivian Communist Party. There was a general awareness in the group; from the time we began our training, we knew that we were being trained to create the first guerrilla *foco* in Bolivia. At no time did we in this group speak of popular insurrection. I repeat, the group was training as a guerrilla force. I believe that Monje took the attitude he did because he aspired to lead the Bolivian group, despite the fact, in the first place, that he knew he had none of the necessary qualifications. Militarily he was useless, he was totally incompetent; he was difficult to get along with and had no real sense militarily of what it meant to be a guerrilla.

Che

As I expected, Monje's attitude was at first evasive, and subsequently treasonous.

The party is already making war on us. I don't know how far it will go, but it will not stop us and in the long run it may even be beneficial; of this, I am almost certain. The most honest and spirited people will remain with us, even though they may pass through crises of conscience of varying degrees of severity.

In the morning, without discussing it with me, Monje informed me that he was leaving and would tend his resignation from the party leadership on January 8th. His mission had ended, according to him. He left looking like a man heading toward the gallows. Inasmuch as his arguments are inconsistent, my impression is that when he learned from Coco of my decision not to give in on strategic matters, he seized on that point to force a rupture.

In the afternoon I got everyone together, explained Monje's attitude and announced that we would unite with all those who wanted to make revolution. I predicted some difficult moments and days of moral anguish for the Bolivians; we would try to solve their problems through collective discussion or meetings with the commissars.

Loyola Guzmán (guerrilla liaison)

This is the first time I have given my impressions of that memorable day for me. Although I knew with whom I was going to meet and for all practical purposes there was no surprise factor, I couldn't help feeling deeply moved; finding myself opposite a comrade like "Ramón" [a pseudonym used by Che in Bolivia] was something I had never expected. He was already a mythical figure, idealized, and suddenly I was facing an uncomplicated, affable man, who despite his fame and prestige didn't make me feel intimidated or inhibited. It was clear he was a highly experienced comrade with an in-depth knowledge of many problems, but this didn't make him authoritarian or despotic. At the time I thought about other leaders of communist parties who look down at us young militants from above and instill us with feelings of inferiority and insignificance. How different comrade "Ramón's" attitude was! It seemed so sincere and genuine to me!

I had a million questions, but I was too excited to ask him anything; my desire to hear directly his opinion on a number of matters remained unfulfilled. When I said goodbye, I felt I was leaving a comrade who had already become very dear to me; at the same time, however, I felt certain that his presence guaranteed the success of the endeavor that was about to begin.

Moisés Guevara was undoubtedly left with the same impression; when he returned to Camiri, he openly expressed his joy and confessed that when he began the trip he didn't think anything serious would come of it. Whatever the situation, he said, he would have been determined to begin the struggle, with only one group, if necessary. But the reality he saw was different from what he expected, and now he was willing to join the struggle unconditionally.

"Ramón" also made reference to the speech he made in Algeria summarizing his own ideas. This document was very important. When he heard that Monje had referred to the presence of foreign comrades in the guerrilla group as a negative and very dangerous factor, comrade "Ramón" replied that this was an example of nationalism that is totally inconsistent with the communist point of view, and that the same thing had occurred in Cuba when the armed struggle began there. Despite it all, the Cuban revolution was victorious.

Strategy and Humanity

Major Rubén Sánchez (Bolivian army officer)
In Camiri, I found that the unit commands, as well as all those who were actually in the zone of operations, were demoralized and afraid.

Che

Stage of consolidation and purging of the guerrilla force, fully accomplished; slow stage of development, incorporating some personnel from Cuba, who don't seem bad, and Guevara's people, who have generally turned out to be very inadequate (two deserters, one prisoner for "talking," three quitters and two weaklings).

Major Rubén Sánchez

We had a guerrilla deserter, "Choque-Choque," in our hands; with the information he gave us, we began to plan our advance on their central camps in Ñancahuazú. I was responsible for the main part of the plan, we could say, approaching their camps from the western part of the ravine. I advanced on the morning of April 4th. I did it so quickly that by midday I was around two hundred meters from the central camp, according to "Choque's" directions.

At that moment, the air force appeared and began to bomb us, confusing us with the guerrillas. Since we were so close to the camp, this had the effect of warning the guerrillas, who dispersed in the surrounding hills. So as soon as the bombing stopped, I entered the camp.

Che

At eight o'clock Rolando reported that there were a dozen soldiers near the ravine we had just abandoned. We left slowly, and at eleven we were already out of danger, on a hilltop.

Major Rubén Sánchez

Entering, you could only see the group and individual positions they had built, probably as sentry posts. Further inside the ravine, in the first camp, I found a sort of kitchen with the embers still hot. In each of these camps—there were three or four—their positions were placed in circular form, not just in one row but in several, moving up the hill. I began to think: I don't believe the guerrillas planned to fight a war of positions, because, according to the theory, the guerrilla force must be agile and dynamic; this must have another purpose.

I found some documents: guard duty assignment lists and a series of other papers that gave us some information; and most important: photographs in which Che appeared. I continued forward; on the other side of the ravine I found the bodies—only skeletons now—of those killed in the first ambush.

Che

When we passed by the ambush site, all that remained of the seven bodies were completely clean skeletons; the birds of prey had done their job well.

Major Rubén Sánchez

On the afternoon of the 9th, I received an order from the Fourth Division to send patrol and reconnaisance missions in three directions: toward the Ñancahuazú Ravine, the village of Gutiérrez and the Iripití region, along the Ñancahuazu River. I planned the operation that night; I ordered Lieutenants Ayala and Lafuente to march along the ravine, and Lieutenant Saavedra to march toward the north.

The following morning, after giving meat and maté to the troops, I ordered them to leave. It was six in the morning.

Che

Morning came and very little happened as we prepared to leave the unpolluted stream and cross along the Miguel Ravine to Pirirenda-Gutiérrez. At mid-morning, El Negro arrived, quite agitated, to tell us that fifteen soldiers were heading toward us, downstream. Inti had gone to our ambush site to warn Rolando. There was nothing we could do but wait, and that's what we did. I sent Tuma, so he would be ready to keep me posted. Soon the first news arrived, and on the balance it was unpleasant: El Rubio—Jesús Suárez Gayol—had been mortally wounded. He was dead upon arrival at our camp, with a bullet in his head.

It happened this way: The ambush party was composed of eight men from the rearguard and a reinforcement of three from the vanguard, spread out on both sides of the river. After telling them about the arrival of the fifteen soldiers, Inti went over to where El Rubio was and saw that he was very poorly positioned; he was clearly visible from the river. The soldiers advanced without taking any particular precautions, scouting the banks of the river for trails. On one of these trails, before falling into the ambush, they encountered Braulio or Pedro. The shooting lasted a few seconds, leaving one dead and three wounded on the spot, plus six or more prisoners; soon afterward, a noncommissioned officer also fell, and four soldiers escaped.

Major Rubén Sánchez

At three in the afternoon, a group of desperate soldiers who had escaped from the Iripití zone appeared. Some of the officers were in such a lamentable state of psychosis that they couldn't explain what had happened. I calmed one of the soldiers down, and he was able to tell me that at eleven in the morning they had a battle with the guerrillas, who ambushed them. He couldn't give me details—distance, number of guerrilla troops—because they got confused and fled, making it back to the camp with great difficulty. Lieutenant Saavedra was killed. I received instructions from Colonel Rocha, Fourth Division commander at the time, to advance. It was already four in the afternoon and it was going to get dark soon, so I moved forward as fast as possible with the thirty-five soldiers I had, plus the eighteen who had returned from the ambush in the morning; I was very concerned about recovering the officer's body.

Che

The following picture emerged from questioning the prisoners: These fifteen men are part of the company that was upstream in Ñancahuazú, had crossed the canyon, recovered the remains of the bodies and then taken the camp. According to the soldiers, they didn't find anything there, although the radio mentioned photos and documents that were found. The company consisted of one hundred men, fifteen of whom brought a group of journalists to our camp. Our prisoners had been sent on a scouting mission and told to return at five p.m. The bulk of the forces are in Pincal, around thirty in Lagunillas, and the group that was in the area of Piraboy, we surmise, has been withdrawn to Gutiérrez.

Major Rubén Sánchez

Instead of withdrawing from the place where they carried out the first ambush, the guerrillas moved two or three kilometers forward and set another one.

Che

Figuring that the soldiers who had escaped would arrive late, I decided that the ambush Rolando had moved forward some five hundred meters should be left in place; this time, however, he could count on the support of the entire vanguard. At first I had ordered a retreat, but then it seemed logical to me to leave them there. When it's nearly 5 p.m., the news arrives that the army is advancing with heavy forces. There is nothing left to do but wait.

Major Rubén Sánchez

Everyone around me was either killed or wounded. Lieutenant Ayala, who was carrying a 60-millimeter mortar, fell wounded, with a bullet in his chest. I alone was left alive, in the midst of the fallen. Then I turned to my left, looking for protection. There I found two soldiers who were also falling back; the enemy front line called on us to surrender. We took up positions and began to shoot toward the area the voices were coming from. At that point another group appears and also demands we surrender. I had one soldier firing to our rear, while the other one and I continued shooting forward. Then the shooting stopped. It grew completely silent. I felt a man's knee on my body; he grabbed my jaw and twisted it.

Che

Scattered gunfire was heard for a while, and Pombo returned to tell us that once again they had fallen into the ambush, several soldiers were killed and a major was taken prisoner.

This time it happened as follows: They moved toward us along the river without taking any great precautions and were completely surprised. This time there are seven dead, five wounded and a total of twenty-two prisoners.

Major Rubén Sánchez

Rolando came down and said to me, "Major, make your troops surrender." "I can't order my people to surrender, I can order them to retreat," I answered. "Make them surrender, because if you don't, we're going to kill them." "Kill me if you want, but I'm not giving the order to surrender."

Rolando went ahead and I stayed with Inti. He offered me a cigarette. "Major, please, don't move from my side," he said. But I couldn't obey him because I had wounded and dead men; one of the wounded was still thrashing about in the water, and I went to help him. Inti saw me and said nothing. When I finished helping the wounded, naturally, I returned to his side.

"You are thieves and murderers," I said to Inti. "Why are you killing my soldiers?" Inti handed me a ring belonging to the lieutenant who had been killed in the morning, and he said: "Take this, give it to his widow; we need the watches. We're neither thieves nor murderers. You call us those names because you don't understand the meaning of our struggle."

When we had calmed down, Inti said to me, "Come here, Major. Let's have a private chat." We were sort of lying down on a bed of dry leaves under a tree and we began to talk. He told me about his life, why he was involved in that struggle, what he had been like as a child, what the guerrillas hoped to achieve, everything. I also told him a lot about myself.

After we had talked for a long while, he brought me alongside a campfire, and a guerrilla named Marcos appears and says, "I found a treasure in the backpack of one of the soldiers: coffee

167

and sugar, gentlemen." They were American rations that we were carrying. "But only the major, myself and the person who makes the coffee are going to drink it," he says. The coffee was made and Marcos said, "No, gentlemen, the major and the wounded are going to drink the coffee." He gave me all the coffee and said, "Drink it, Major, you must be tired and wet." And I drank the coffee.

Che

In the morning we began to move all our gear, and we buried Rubio in a shallow grave, given our lack of materials. Inti was left with the rearguard to escort the prisoners and set them free, as well as to look for more weapons scattered in the area. The only result of the search was to take two new prisoners with their respective Garands. We gave two copies of war dispatch Number One to the major, who promised to get it to the media. The total number of losses was as follows: ten dead, including two lieutenants; thirty prisoners (a major, a few noncommissioned officers and the rest soldiers); six wounded (one in the first battle and the rest in the second).

Major Rubén Sánchez

I was invited to stay with the guerrillas, but I didn't accept. I told them I couldn't be a traitor and I still didn't fully understand the guerrillas' goals. They gave me a communiqué, which I delivered to the press, as I had promised.

Naturally, I began to analyze the guerrillas' arguments in-depth. I read Régis Debray's book, *Revolution in the Revolution?*, and other texts. I took a growing interest in those books, which were so closely related to my feelings on social issues. Hey, I thought, I'm going to give everything I've got to this struggle.*

*Major Rubén Sánchez was commander of the Colorado Regiment, which fought against the 1971 fascist coup in Bolivia, and was the last officer loyal to General Juan José Torres.

Definitions

Carlos María Gutiérrez (Uruguayan journalist)

I didn't realize that my professional vices were bothering him. He didn't want to hear anything about his being a guerrilla hero, and he resented my feeling that I had a right, just because I am a journalist, to ask anything I wanted to satisfy my curiosity. There we were, two guys drinking coffee in the sun, and up to that point the only things we found in common were an interest in photography and a liking for certain places we both had visited. Everything else—the past, plans, dreams, the future— are things that are discussed among friends, and no one could interfere in his business unless you enjoyed that status, which I didn't.

He defended himself with abrupt sarcasm and a silent smile; they were the tools with which he examined me as if to evaluate my impertinence or ingenuousness. Che knew how to build his "fortifications" and handle his "drawbridges."

But he also was intuitively cordial, and his abruptness left no wounds once one understood that it was all part of an obsessive desire to be sincere at all times, that frankness was Che's basic creed. With his Buenos Aires sarcasm, he tore down my pretentiousness, my pedantic references to doctrines or ideas, the Uruguayan seriousness with which I attempted to situate a struggle he was waging—with his debilitated body, his asthma and his blood—on a purely historical or political-ideological plane.

Later, when I shut my notebook, disconcerted and still bewildered, he took a step in the direction he wished to lead me and lowered a "drawbridge": "When you go, could you take a letter for my mother in Buenos Aires?"

Ezequiel Martínez Estrada (Argentinian writer)

When he appeared in public, under the spotlights, the assembly broke into effusive applause, demonstrating the fervor that Guevara has roused among young people. I listened to him intently and critically to see what in his words and gestures could be regarded as show, since the big media presents him, as they do Fidel Castro, as a demagogical mystic. I've had some experience with that sort of democratic pretender—an indigenous product of our lands—and a certain knowledge of the tricks of the trade. My position was one of wary sympathy. He spoke calmly, without gesticulating and without pathos in his voice, neither exaggerating nor using familiar oratorical images. He spoke confidently and knowledgeably, addressing himself not to an auditorium, but to a large family: plainly, with dignity.

Enrique Oltuski

One day I put my hand on his shoulder as a sign of affection, and he said, "And this familiarity?. . ." And I dropped my hand.

Time passed, and one day he said to me, "Do you know what? You're not such a son of a bitch as they told me." And we laughed and became friends.

One time I asked him, "Haven't you ever been afraid?" And he answered, "Incredibly afraid."

Ezequiel Martínez Estrada

For me, tired and far from my country, the opportunity I had sometime later to converse with the person I, too, can call Che Guevara was uplifting.

What did we talk about? About Argentina, about people, places and things we both knew and are where they always were. We have both preserved an unstained flag from there that we can unfurl wherever we are. Che Guevara makes me feel that I too can do something for my forgotten brothers and children, wherever fate leads me. The desk is covered with papers; on a small table there is a maté gourd with metal straws, a sort of good-luck charm that only moves the initiated. Rubén Darío called it the "peace pipe," because people drink out of it collectively. It is a symbol of friendship.

The maté, which unfailingly accompanies us when we have left our homeland, is the last remaining thing that preserves for the palate the taste of our native land. We know each other without having met. We converse the same way we drink maté; there is no imbalance between his height and my smallness. We are together, side by side, talking as equals, because our status as huumans takes precedence over the rest. I relax in his company. Imperceptibly, the conversation takes on a confidential tone, and without warning we find ourselves exchanging memories as if they were tokens of friendship. I listen to a man of inherent sincerity, uncomplicated and candid, who captivates you with his devotion and inspires confidence. Guevara has forgotten how much he has learned and knows, and he is living anew a life that isn't his. Let's hope I can do the same.

The nation that calls him Che Guevara doesn't know that in Guaraní it means *my* Guevara. In effect, he is part of the people and has regenerated himself by devoting himself to the people. Fleeing, like Jonah, he has fulfilled an imperative task. The hand that guides him on his path is manifest. He helps me join him; this man who could be my son takes me by the arm, paternally, as if he were carrying out a mission to protect and give me counsel.

This is how we say goodbye, without separating. I look at him steadfastly so I won't forget him; I take in his whole Judas Maccabeus face, and I feel an energy in my arm that makes me feel freer and more resolute. I understand that I should tell as best and as accurately as I can what has been revealed to me. I will fulfill this obligation until the end. I tell him: There are many lives in your hands, and you are also in the hands of another; the hands of the good Lord, who is served—whether they know it or not—by all those who fight the tyrants.

Stephanie Harrington (U.S. journalist)

He finally arrived, an hour and a half late. There was an uncomfortable silence in the room. It was one of those annoying moments in a gathering when no one knows how to break the

silence. Everyone—all those brilliant, influential and sophisti-
cated people—was momentarily speechless, almost lifeless, as if
they had turned into pillars of salt, like Lot's wife, for having
contemplated the forbidden. After all, when the subject of our
daydreams enters the room, we can't help being impressed.

At times like those it becomes hard even to say something
polite. Ernesto Che Guevara appeared in immaculate and well-
pressed fatigues. He and his interpreter were introduced to the
guests by the host, *Look* correspondent Laura Bergquist, whose
career in journalism had brought her into contact with a large
number of Latin American leaders, and who had borrowed her
friend Bobo Rockefeller's house because it was located only a few
yards from the Cuban embassy.

The ice was broken by one of those aggressive types who can
overcome any inhibition in order to shake a famous person's
hand. A few embarrassing minutes passed until Guevara finally
sat down on a sofa and the guests found the courage to speak to
him.

After cocktails, dinner was served at several tables covered
with red tablecloths. Sitting at the tables were a number of
eminent figures: writers, television producers, a priest (liberal,
of course), as well as I. F. Stone, Jack Gelber, Lisa Howard, Lucy
Jarvis and Nat Hentoff. There were a number of sincere toasts in
honor of the Cuban revolution and some that were less sincere,
emphasizing the few prevailing civil liberties on the island.
Jimmy Wechsler, one of those who felt a mixture of admiration
and mistrust toward Guevara, had the good taste to avoid that
type of conversation.

After dinner, the wine and the toasts, the conversation began
to flow, but in short, stale drifts, the usual answers to the usual
questions. Bill Strickland, then a leader of the student movement, asked Guevara how U.S. students could emulate Castro
in the Sierra Maestra and organize guerrilla activity here.
Guevara laughed, and explained courteously that the situation
here was somewhat different, and he didn't believe that urban
North American was a setting in which tactics of that sort would
be successful.

The rest of the evening was amusing but strangely unreal. Strangest of all was that no one could figure out what Guevara was doing there, not only in that room, but in the country. Aside from his fatigues, he was there like any other guest, well-equipped with his middle-class Argentinian education.

Hernán Benítez (priest)

To have spent his life in the jungle, hungry and naked, with a price-tag (of fifteen thousand dollars!) on his head, confronting the military power of imperialism, and as if this weren't enough, being sick with asthma, exposing himself to the possibility of choking to death if the bullets didn't cut him down... He, who could have lived comfortably, with money, fun, friends, women and vices in any of the great cities of sin... This is heroism, true heroism, as confused as his ideas may have been. Not to recognize this is not merely reactionary; it is stupid.

Dona Celia de la Serna de Guevara (mother)

I would like to see him walk down this damp, dark street. I wish he could walk through this city again; pass by the child splashing in the mud of the shantytown; feel the anger that has built up, without people knowing why, over the yoke of the ten-hour day; see, as I do now, the melancholy pair of blows in which a sad romance in the park comes to an end; speak with the furniture maker who sold his last chair to make his last meal; bear the burden of dignified misery of the teacher who earns three thousand pesos and wears a cheap cotton smock; go to Viedma where there are people who have been tortured; know Mrs. Ahumada and her martyrdom; be among us once again. Then, I am certain, someone would stretch out a large, thick, dark hand, and would, perhaps, say, "We are ready, my commander!"